MR. LINCOLN'S
INAUGURAL JOURNEY

☆☆☆☆☆☆☆☆☆

MR. LINCOLN'S INAUGURAL JOURNEY

☆☆☆☆☆☆☆☆

BY MARY KAY PHELAN

DRAWINGS BY RICHARD CUFFARI

THOMAS Y. CROWELL COMPANY NEW YORK

Designed by Jill Schwartz

Manufactured in the United States of America

L.C. Card 76–175110
ISBN 0-690-54526-6
   2 3 4 5 6 7 8 9 10

Especially for

Marty, Jerry, Edna, and Dick

By the Author

Acknowledgments

The author would like to state that this narrative of *Mr. Lincoln's Inaugural Journey* is a true account, based on firsthand sources—newspapers, diaries, journals, and interviews reported by contemporaries. No conversations have been invented or fictionized.

Two volumes in particular were especially helpful in the preparation of this book: *The Collected Works of Abraham Lincoln,* Volume IV, edited by Roy P. Basler, and *Lincoln and the Baltimore Plot,* edited by Norma B. Cuthbert. The newspapers for February 1861 were also invaluable.

Contents

MR. LINCOLN'S INAUGURAL JOURNEY

☆☆☆☆☆☆☆☆☆

1 THE UNION DISSOLVING
⋆ Sunday, February 10, 1861 ⋆

Ominous clouds hover overhead, and there's a damp chill in the air on this bleak Sunday morning. The sprawling community of Springfield, Illinois, has been experiencing unseasonably warm weather the past few days. Last night's downpour left the muddy streets dotted with puddles. And now more rain is predicted.

For President-elect Abraham Lincoln this is the last day he will spend in the little Illinois capital of 9,320 inhabitants—the town which has been his home and where he has practiced law for the past sixteen years. Tomorrow begins the thirteen-day inaugural journey to Washington, D.C.

The length of the trip is a purely personal choice on Mr. Lincoln's part. He could have reached the nation's capital in two or three days. But the raw-boned prairie lawyer is little known beyond his own state. He wants to show himself to the nation that elected him—to let the people see him, shake his hand, give them a chance to hear him speak.

The long and circuitous route he has selected will carry the President-elect to overnight stops in Indianapolis, Cincinnati, Columbus, Pittsburgh, Cleveland, Buffalo, Albany, New York City, Philadelphia, and Harrisburg. There will be whistle-stops, too, at many small towns along the way.

For the past eight months the town of Springfield has seethed with excitement—ever since last May when its most prominent citizen was nominated by the Republican party for the United States Presidency. A constant flow of visitors poured into the town, and Mr. Lincoln accepted the governor's offer to use his office in the sandstone statehouse on the public square. This, everyone agreed, was a more suitable place in which to greet the large numbers who came to talk with the nominee.

The Republicans had drawn up a three-point platform at their national convention in Chicago. First, slavery would not be disturbed in those states where slaveholding was already legal, but it must be kept out of the territories—those western lands belonging to the United States that had yet to be admitted to statehood. Second, American industries are to be protected by placing higher tariffs on goods imported from other countries; and third, free homestead land is to be distributed to those wishing to move farther west.

The Republican nominee has endorsed this platform wholeheartedly. The most vital issue in it was, of course, the plank on slavery. And as the months passed, the Southerners became more and more alarmed. If Lincoln should win the national election, the slave states threatened to withdraw from the Union and set up their own government.

Republican politicians pleaded with Mr. Lincoln to reassure the "honestly alarmed men" over the slavery turmoil in the South, but the nominee contended there were no such men. "It is the trick by which the South breaks down every Northern man," he said. "If I yielded to their entreaties, I would go to Washington without the support of the men who now support me. I would be as powerless as a block of buckeye wood. The honest men . . . will find in our platform everything I could say now, or which they would ask me to say."

The growing unrest in the country was reflected in the market baskets of mail delivered to Mr. Lincoln each morning from the local post office. Letters came from even remote corners of the nation. The nominee tried to read each one himself and to answer in longhand as many as possible.

One communication, however, gave Mr. Lincoln special pleasure. It came from Grace Bedell in Westfield, New York. In part she wrote: "I am a little girl only eleven years old, but want you should be President of the United States very much so I hope you won't think me very bold to write to such a great man as you are." After inquiring whether Mr. Lincoln had any little girls, she added: "If you will let your whiskers grow . . . you would look a great deal better for your face is so thin. All the ladies like whiskers and they would tease their husbands to vote for you and then you would be President."

Mr. Lincoln answered his young correspondent immediately, writing in a painstaking hand:

Private

Springfield, Ill.
Oct. 19, 1860

Miss Grace Bedell
My dear little Miss,

Your very agreeable letter of the 15th is received.

I regret the necessity of saying I have no daughter. I have three sons—one seventeen, one nine, and one seven years of age. They, with their mother, constitute my whole family.

As to the whiskers, having never worn any, do you not think people would call it a piece of silly affection if I were to begin it now?

Your very sincere well-wisher
A. Lincoln

A few weeks later, the nominee changed his mind about a beard being "a piece of silly affection." He began letting his chin whiskers sprout, and when his barber, William Florville, sharpened his razor to shave them off, Mr. Lincoln said, "Billy, let's give them a chance to grow."

Now on this eve of departure from Springfield, the President-elect has a full beard—more flattering, perhaps, though it scarcely conceals the worry that lines his thin face.

The news of Mr. Lincoln's election to the Presidency last November sixth was cause for great

celebration in Springfield. A few days later, a special correspondent for the *New York Tribune* came to the town. On November 14, 1860, his appraisal of the newly elected President appeared in that paper:

> Mr. Lincoln's regular habits are not in the slightest degree changed since the assurance of his election to the Presidency. Without showing anything like indifference to his new honors, he bears them so quietly and easily as to prove the dignity of his high office will not weigh at all oppressively upon him. . . . Mr. Lincoln is no more unduly elated by his success than he would have been unduly depressed in case of defeat. He is precisely the same man as before—open and generous in his personal communication with all who approach him, though reticent enough, for the present as regards his political intentions.

After the election, secessionist turmoil increased throughout the South. Again many people implored the President-elect to say something that would placate the Southerners. But he remained silent, resolving not "to write or speak anything upon doctrinal points." In a confidential letter to Alexander Stephens of Georgia, Mr. Lincoln reduced the differences between North and South to a single sentence: "You think slavery is *right*," he wrote, "and ought to be extended; while we think it is *wrong* and ought to be restricted."

Just last December 20 the Southern tempest reached a climax. South Carolina by unanimous vote in convention seceded from the Union. Mississippi, Florida, Alabama, Georgia, Louisiana, and Texas followed. In these states the Stars and

Stripes were hauled down. Armed citizens in the new republic of Louisiana seized the United States Mint and Customs House in New Orleans. Angry Floridians plundered the Pensacola navy yard. In Texas all federal forts were confiscated by the state; arms, ammunition, and equipment were seized.

During the past three months Mr. Lincoln has been caught up in a whirlwind of activity, as a brilliant young newsman, Henry Villard of the *New York Herald,* has reported to his paper. When he first arrived, Villard was astonished at the number of "motley" visitors who came to Springfield. He wrote:

> Everybody that lives in this vicinity or passes through this place goes to take a look at Old Abe. Muddy boots and hickory shirts are just as frequent as broadcloth, fine linen, etc. The ladies, however, are usually dressed up in their very best, although they cannot hope to make an impression on old married Lincoln.

Officeseekers and visitors besieged the President-elect. He listened to advice about what men he should appoint to his Cabinet. He conferred for hours with anxious Northern and Southern leaders, hoping desperately that a break between the two factions can be avoided. Eight of the fifteen slave states still remain in the Union. If only they can be kept from seceding, perhaps those who have formed the Confederacy will reconsider their drastic action.

Mail continued to pour into Mr. Lincoln's office. Among the many letters have been anonymous threats on the life of the President-elect. Funeral wreaths, pictures of coffins, drawings of skulls and crossbones on black-bordered stationery, arrived almost daily.

There have been frightening hints, too, about the fate of the national capital. Last Christmas Day the Richmond *Enquirer* asked its readers:

> . . . if the Governor of Maryland, influenced by timidity or actuated by treachery, shall longer delay to permit the people of that State to protect themselves, can there not be found men bold and brave enough to unite with Virginians in seizing the capitol at Washington and the Federal defenses within the two states?

On December 29, Senator William H. Seward of New York wrote to Mr. Lincoln from Washington:

> A plot is forming to seize the capital on or before the 4th of March, and this, too, has its accomplices in the public councils. I could tell you more particularly than I dare write, but you must not imagine that I am giving you suspicions and rumors. Believe me, I know what I write!

The President-elect has remained calm, despite the many rumors and threats. At the urging of friends, he did, however, decide late last month to send Thomas S. Mather, adjutant general of Illinois, to Washington, D.C., on a special mission. Mather was to visit General Winfield Scott, commander of the United States Army, and learn what steps had been taken to insure an orderly inauguration. The President-elect also wanted to make certain that the general was "really and unreservedly" a Union man.

General Scott was ill when Mather came to call, but he was nonetheless vehement in his expressions of loyalty. "You may present my compliments to Mr. Lincoln when you reach Springfield," said Scott, "and tell him that I shall expect him to come on to Washington as soon as he is ready.

"Say to him, also, that when once here, I shall consider myself responsible for his safety. If necessary, I shall plant cannon at both ends of Pennsylvania Avenue and if any of the Maryland or Virginia gentlemen who have become so threatening and troublesome of late, show their heads, or even venture to raise a finger, I shall blow them to Hell."

When Mather returned to Springfield, he reported these exact words to the President-elect. Thus reassured, Mr. Lincoln is now confident that there is no need for alarm.

Mr. Lincoln's Journey

Springfield, Illinois — Washington, D.C.

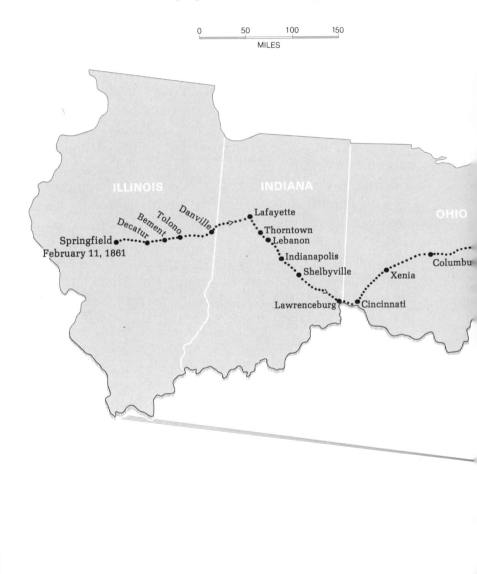

Rochester

Buffalo

Syracuse

Troy

Schenectady
Albany

NEW YORK

Dunkirk
Westfield

Girard

Poughkeepsie

Cleveland

Peekskill

Ravenna

Alliance

Jersey City
Newark
Elizabeth
Rahway

PENNSYLVANIA

Wellsville

ubenville

Pittsburgh

New York City

Princeton
Trenton

Freedom

Harrisburg

Elizabethtown

NEW

Lancaster

Philadelphia

JERSEY

MARYLAND

Baltimore

Washington, D.C.
February 23, 1861

United States in 1861

mp

2 TIME TO REMEMBER
⋆ Sunday, February 10, 1861 ⋆

Despite the press of activity, Mr. Lincoln found time to slip away and work on his inaugural address. Now, thankfully, it is finished. At odd hours for the last several weeks, he has secreted himself in the dusty storeroom above the dry-goods store owned by his brother-in-law, C. M. Smith.

Before beginning work on the manuscript, Mr. Lincoln asked his junior law partner, William Herndon, to collect several volumes he wanted for reference. Herndon was surprised by the list the President-elect handed him. There were only four items: a copy of the United States Constitution, Andrew Jackson's Proclamation against Nullification, which asserted the federal government's right to take action against any state that attempted to set aside federal law; Henry Clay's famous speech on the Compromise of 1850; and Daniel Webster's reply to Robert Hayne in their debate over the growth of federal power.

Once the manuscript was completed, it was set

in type by Lincoln's good friend, William H. Bailhache, co-owner of the *Illinois State Journal*. Knowing how important it was that the address be kept
from prying eyes, Mr. Bailhache locked himself
in the printing room for an entire weekend. He
struck off only twenty copies and then broke up
the type forms. Now the precious papers are
packed in the black oilcloth gripsack that is to be
carried by hand on the journey to Washington.

In the gripsack, too, have been placed envelopes
containing notes for the speeches that will be delivered en route. Each envelope is carefully labeled
with the name of the city where a major address
is scheduled. Mr. Lincoln made these notes while
Thomas D. Jones, an Ohio sculptor, worked on a
clay bust of the President-elect.

Jones had set up a temporary studio in a room at
the St. Nicholas Hotel, and for an hour each day,
starting in late December, Mr. Lincoln came to the
studio. There, while the sculptor attempted to cap-
ture the deep-set eyes, the gaunt, bony facial
structure, the kindly expression of his subject, the
President-elect sat with a small portfolio on his
knees. Using blue-ruled paper, he would jot down
notes, often referring to copies of his published
speeches. Jones reported that once Mr. Lincoln
finished a manuscript, "he would modestly read it
to me."

There's little doubt that these past few weeks
have been hectic ones. In addition to the line of
callers and the deluge of mail, personal prepara-

tions have had to be made for moving the family
to Washington. The two-story frame dwelling at
the corner of Eighth and Jackson—the home
where the Lincolns lived for the last seventeen
years—was rented to Lucian Tilton, president of
the Great Western Railway. S. H. Melvin, a local
druggist, bought the household goods advertised
"for private sale . . . without reserve" in the *Illinois State Journal.* The black nameplate on the
front door, with "A. Lincoln" etched in Roman letters, has been removed.

Last Wednesday evening the President-elect
and Mrs. Lincoln held a reception to bid farewell
to their Springfield friends. Seven hundred people
responded to the newspaper invitation. According
to one guest, "It took twenty minutes to get in the
hall door. And then it required no little manage-
ment to make your way out."

The following morning the Lincoln family
moved to the recently remodeled Chenery House
on West Washington Street to spend their few
remaining days in Springfield. Because the inaugural journey will be a long one, Mr. Lincoln suggested that his wife and two younger sons, Tad
and Willie, remain here after he leaves. Rather
than subject them to the tedium of the lengthy
trip, he wants them to join the inaugural train in
New York City.

Seventeen-year-old Robert, a freshman this year
at Harvard, returned home several weeks ago. He
will accompany his father when the Presidential

party leaves tomorrow. At the moment Mrs. Lincoln is wondering how she will ever be able to keep within bounds seven-year-old Tad—her "little troublesome sunshine"—and his nine-year-old brother, Willie. They are continually getting into mischief in the hotel.

On this final Sunday in Springfield, Mr. Lincoln has been chatting with his closest political friends. About mid-afternoon he excuses himself and walks across the street to a store building on the west side of the public square. Slowly he climbs the unbanistered wooden stairway that leads to a dingy back room on the second floor. It is here that he and William Herndon, fourteen years his junior, have practiced law together.

As he opens the door, Mr. Lincoln studies his partner seated at the round pine table in the center of the room. It's all so familiar—the well-worn horsehair sofa along the south wall, the small two-drawer desk on the opposite wall with a bookcase mounted above. Assorted volumes of law books and statistical reports fill the three lower shelves, while pamphlets, legal documents, and letters are scattered on the two shelves above. On top of the bookcase is a pasteboard box containing bundles of letters and papers neatly tied. Some time ago Mr. Lincoln inscribed a cryptic message on one of these packages: "When you can't find it anywhere else, look into this."

For the next hour or so, Mr. Lincoln and William Herndon confer about business. It's been

more than seven months since the President-elect has been able to practice law, and arrangements must be made for settling some unfinished matters. There are a number of cases in which Mr. Lincoln is particularly interested. For these he suggests certain procedures which he hopes Herndon will follow.

After they finish, the President-elect crosses over to the old sofa and stretches out his lanky frame in a position he has taken hundreds of times.

For a few moments Mr. Lincoln is silent, running his bony fingers through his tousled hair. He stares absentmindedly at the ceiling, begrimed with smoke from the rusty wood-burning stove in the corner.

The room holds many memories. Here in this stuffy little office he has known both defeat and success. Here he has worked on law cases and argued for hours about states' rights and secession, slavery and abolition—the very issues leading to the national crisis that he has been called upon to avert.

Presently Mr. Lincoln turns his head toward his partner. "Billy," he inquires, "how long have we been together?"

"Over sixteen years," Herndon replies.

"We've never had a cross word during all that time, have we?"

"No indeed," his partner says.

Again fixing his gaze on the ceiling, Mr. Lincoln begins recalling the adventures of their early days together. Herndon has never seen his partner in a more cheerful mood. For the next hour or so, the two men share reminiscences of people and places they have known.

At the conclusion of their talk, Mr. Lincoln eases his lanky frame up to a standing position and gathers up a bundle of personal papers. Opening the door, he glances down the stairway at the old "Lincoln & Herndon" signboard swinging on its rusty hinges.

"Let it hang there undisturbed," he urges in a low voice. "Give our clients to understand that the election of a President makes no change in the firm of Lincoln & Herndon; for if I live, I'm coming back in due time, and then we'll resume practice as if nothing happened."

train from Chicago to Baltimore, accompanied by three of his operatives: Timothy Webster, Harry Davies, and Mrs. Kate Warne. He deliberately chose Baltimore for his headquarters, because it is here that the rumors have been most persistent. On many occasions threats have been freely voiced that "No damned abolitionist should be allowed to pass through the town alive." Furthermore, this is the only city sympathetic to the South through which Mr. Lincoln will travel en route to Washington, D.C. The detective believed it very possible that trouble might occur here.

Baltimore's police department is headed by Marshal George P. Kane, well known as a staunch secessionist; the men on his force are, without exception, sympathetic to the Southern cause. Under Kane, the police have made no effort to subdue those intent on spreading suspicion, discontent, and hatred toward the North. In many instances, they have even openly assisted those individuals who hoped to cause trouble. Furthermore, Baltimore has planned no reception for the President-elect; no parade will march through the city, such as has been scheduled for every other stopover. This fact in itself seemed disturbing to the detective.

After Pinkerton and his operatives arrived in Baltimore, Timothy Webster was sent to Perrymansville, about nine miles south of Havre de Grace, Maryland. There have been reports that a rebel cavalry company was organizing there, and

Webster was told to infiltrate their group, if possible, and learn what he could about plots to destroy the ferry.

Operatives Harry Davies and Mrs. Kate Warne checked in at Barnum's Hotel, reputed to be the favorite hostelry of Southern visitors. Mrs. Warne, under the name of Mrs. Cherry, is to play the role of a wealthy gentlewoman from Montgomery, Alabama, sympathetic to the secessionist cause. Pinkerton, who knows she is both a brilliant conversationalist and a good listener, has advised her to strike up friendships with the wives of Southern men staying at the hotel and glean whatever information she can. Davies is posing as Joseph Howard, the son of a wealthy plantation owner from New Orleans. He is to frequent the bar at Barnum's Hotel, report everything he overhears, and try to find out who the leaders of the secessionist groups are.

Pinkerton himself decided to assume the alias of John H. Hutchinson, a Southerner who is very vocal about his hatred for the federal government. He has rented a building on South Street and set himself up in business as a broker. The office should suit his purposes admirably; entrance can be made from any of its four sides because of the alleyways that lead in from neighboring streets. Thus, his operatives can come and go without arousing suspicion. In the guise of a man dealing in stocks and bonds, the detective has made it a practice to listen to as many conversa-

tions as possible—in hotel lobbies, barber shops, billiard rooms, and bars.

During their first week in Baltimore the agents brought Pinkerton much information, but most of it was routine and indefinite. Yet from the many rumors they gathered, he has been able to determine that the mood of the city is indeed dangerous. In all kinds of neighborhoods, rich as well as poor, there have been frequent clashes between partisans of the North and South. Such fierce sentiments, the chief concluded, might easily lead to extreme violence.

Harry Davies has managed to gain the confidence of a local resident, O. K. Hillard, a wealthy aristocrat who apparently is involved with a pro-Southern group. The nominal leader of this group is an Italian named Cypriano Ferrandina, the head barber at Barnum's Hotel.

Ferrandina first came to Baltimore some ten years ago, and in recent months he has made no secret of his hatred for Abraham Lincoln. Davies, however, has not yet been able to pinpoint any firm details about the plans of the group. Down in Perrymansville, Operative Webster has been accepted in the cavalry company. There has been much talk, but he still has not uncovered any real conspiracy to blow up the ferry and cripple the railroad.

Night after night the chief detective has pored over the reports of his agents, hoping to find some clue, some indication of a plot. But until today nothing has turned up. There has only been the grim and persistent rumor that Abraham Lincoln will never be allowed to reach Washington, D.C., alive. Never.

Pinkerton has studied thoroughly the published schedule of Mr. Lincoln's itinerary. The President-elect is to arrive from Harrisburg at Baltimore's Calvert Street Station on Saturday, February 23, at 12:30 P.M. From there he will be escorted through a narrow pedestrian tunnel to the point where carriages will be waiting. The Presidential party is then to drive to the Eutaw House, change carriages, and proceed to the Camden Street Station where they will board a Baltimore and Ohio Railroad train for Washington, D.C.

Within the past few days Chief Kane has publicly stated that he has no special police to spare for Mr. Lincoln's arrival. He will try and scrape up a few men to cover the Calvert Street Station, but he can guarantee nothing. Pinkerton knows that the narrow tunnel will be filled with people who want to take a look at the President-elect. Here is a real danger point; he does not like the situation at all.

Now on this dreary Sunday afternoon while the President-elect is bidding good-bye to old friends in Springfield, Allan Pinkerton has just received word from an official of the Philadelphia, Wilmington and Baltimore Railroad. William Stearns, the master mechanic, has uncovered evidence of an actual plot to kill the President-elect before he

arrives in the national capital. "They may attempt
to do it while he is passing over our line," Stearns
has warned. Pinkerton's mind races through the
possibilities of how best to handle this alarming
situation.

He is well acquainted with the Honorable Norman P. Judd, who will accompany Mr. Lincoln
during the thirteen-day inaugural journey. Knowing that Judd is a close personal friend of the
President-elect, Pinkerton decides to inform him.
There is no time now to get word to Springfield
before the party leaves. He determines to work
through his home office in Chicago. George H.
Bangs, his agency chief, will be able to coordinate
the details.

Since the Presidential party will arrive in Indianapolis tomorrow night, a wire can be sent to
Judd there, asking where a personal messenger can
deliver a letter too important to be trusted to the
mails. After scribbling out the telegram, Pinkerton
begins writing the news. He doesn't yet know
any details about the conspiracy, he tells Judd, but
he is convinced that a very real threat exists to the
life of the President-elect. There will be no effort
spared to ferret out the plot. He advises Judd to
confide in no one but to be alert for further communications.

Placing both the wire and the letter in an envelope addressed to Mr. Bangs, he adds a lengthy
note of explanation. Bangs is to send the wire
immediately and await Judd's reply. Then, he

should instruct the messenger where the letter is to be delivered. After signing his name, Pinkerton rechecks every angle. Has he overlooked anything? Satisfied, he seals the envelope. Throwing on his greatcoat, the detective hurries out through the chill twilight to post the communications to his Chicago office.

4 FAREWELL TO SPRINGFIELD
★ Monday, February 11, 1861 ★

An icy mist is falling when the President-elect arises at an early hour. The sky is overcast, and the dismal weather only heightens the depression Mr. Lincoln feels on this his last morning in Springfield. Nevertheless, there is one final detail to which he must attend. He hustles down to the hotel office where the family's personal trunks are collected. Drawing out a coil of rope from his pocket, he begins tying up the trunks. Once the job is completed, Mr. Lincoln takes several hotel cards, and on the back of each he writes:

> A. Lincoln
> White House
> Washington, D.C.

From a nearby corner the landlord's daughter watches as the President-elect tacks the cards on the trunks. Hesitantly she steps forward and asks Mr. Lincoln for his autograph. He smiles at the little girl, takes another hotel card, and scrawls his name across the back.

Returning to the family's suite of rooms, he finds everyone ready. Mrs. Lincoln, Willie, and Tad will come with him to the station, although only Robert will accompany his father on today's train ride. Mr. Lincoln picks up the black gripsack that contains his inaugural address, as well as the speech notes for the major stops. Without revealing its contents, he hands the bag to Robert, asking him to watch over it during the journey.

Promptly at half past seven, the Chenery House omnibus backs up in front of the hotel entrance. The trunks are loaded, and the family climbs aboard the horse-drawn vehicle. The clop-clop of hoofs echoes through the street as the omnibus heads for the Great Western railroad station several blocks away.

For the past two hours people have been gathering at the little brick depot. Mr. Lincoln has asked that there be no celebration. Only last night he told reporters questioning him in the hotel lobby that he did not intend to make a speech. Yet, despite the weather and the early hour, the dingy waiting room is filled with friends, neighbors, and constituents. The crowd has grown until there is no more room even under the wide eaves that extend out over the platform. Latecomers are standing in the rain, many holding umbrellas over their heads. More than a thousand people have come to pay tribute to their famous townsman as he departs for Washington, D.C.

When the omnibus halts at the depot, the trunks

are unloaded; Mr. Lincoln and his family make their way into the waiting room. The well-wishers file quietly by for a final handshake. Some say a few words of farewell; others are overcome by emotion and merely press Mr. Lincoln's hand.

On the railroad track beside the depot the Presidential Special is ready for departure. Heading the train is the stubby locomotive, *L. M. Wiley*—its brasswork glistening, its pointed cowcatcher decorated with American flags, now sodden and limp in the morning damp. Smoke pours from the engine's huge balloon stack; cordwood has been piled on the tender. Behind the locomotive are two cars—a passenger coach and a baggage car—both vividly colored. The wooden panels of the cars have been painted a bright orange, splashed with flourishes of black and varnished to a high gleam.

The interior of the passenger coach has been specially decorated for the inaugural journey. The walls are covered with crimson plush; red, white, and blue festoons hang from the molding. Draped between the windows is heavy blue silk studded with thirty-four silver stars, one for each state. The furniture is dark mahogany, contrasting effectively with the light-colored tapestry carpet. At either end of the car two American flags are crossed above the doorway.

In charge of the entire journey is William S. Wood, whose title is "Superintendent of Arrangements." A former Eastern railroad official, he was recommended to Mr. Lincoln by Thurlow Weed, a Republican leader in New York State. Wood's assistant is Burnett Forbes. He will escort Mrs. Lincoln, Willie, and Tad when they leave to join the President-elect later. Thc President-elect has also asked William Johnson, a Springfield Negro whom he has known and liked for many years, to accompany his family. Mr. Lincoln hopes to employ Johnson as his valet and private messenger after he moves into the White House.

Just last week Mr. Wood returned to Springfield from an inspection tour of the entire route. He consulted at length with railroad officials. Then he issued complete timetables and operating instructions to those lines that will participate in the inaugural journey. He has had handbills printed giving carriage protocol for the local welcoming committees; he has carefully listed those who are authorized to travel in the Presidential party. Both instructions and passenger lists have been mailed to all the public officials involved, as well as to newspapers throughout the country. The schedule has already been well publicized.

With the exception of the President-elect and his son Robert, the official party is already on board. Included among them is George Latham, Robert's boyhood friend from Springfield who is now a student at Yale; Dr. W. S. Wallace, Mr. Lincoln's personal physician as well as his brother-in-law; and Robert Irwin, his financial adviser.

Acting as private secretary is John Nicolay, a

young German educated in the United States. Slim, pale, and good-looking, he was formerly in the office of the Illinois secretary of state. Because of his intelligence, industry, and discretion, he became invaluable to Mr. Lincoln last fall. Now he has accepted the secretarial post with obvious pride. Assisting him is young John M. Hay, a graduate of Brown College and a lawyer only recently admitted to the Illinois bar.

Perhaps the most prominent person in the party, other than the President-elect, is Colonel Elmer Ephraim Ellsworth, a twenty-three-year-old officer who heads the United States Zouave Cadets. The Zouaves are a volunteer marching organization that has achieved national fame. On a tour last year they made such a favorable impression that Zouave marching groups have sprung up all over the country.

A reporter for the *New York Sunday Mercury* has written:

> A fellow who can climb an 80-foot rope, hand over hand, with a barrel of flour hanging to his heels; who can set a 40-foot ladder on end, balance himself on top of it and shoot wild pigeons on the wing, one at a time, just behind the eye; who can take a five-shooting revolver in each hand and knock the spots out of the ten of diamonds at 80 paces, turning somersaults all the time and firing every shot in the air— that is a Zouave.

The handsome young colonel (whose honorary title is self-imposed) first came to Springfield to read law in the office of Lincoln & Herndon. He is devoted to Mr. Lincoln, and the affection is returned; Ellsworth has become almost like a son. The older man and the younger have been, as Mr. Lincoln put it, "as intimate as the disparity of our ages and my engrossing engagements will permit." The President-elect has invited Ellsworth to accompany the party as his aide.

Acting in a protective role, also, is the barrel-chested Colonel Ward Hill Lamon. He was a law partner of the President-elect from 1852 to 1856 when Mr. Lincoln maintained a law office in Danville, Illinois. They rode the eighth judicial circuit together and developed a lasting friendship, though people sometimes wondered at the attachment between the blustering Lamon and the gentle-mannered Mr. Lincoln. Today Lamon is wearing a handsome uniform which he designed himself when he was appointed aide to the governor of Illinois.

The War Department has detailed four army officers to ride the Special and guard the President-elect: Colonel E. V. Sumner, Major David Hunter, Captain George W. Hazzard, and Captain John Pope. However routine the gesture may be, the officers take their duties very seriously. Hunter, Hazzard, and Pope are on the train this morning; Colonel Sumner plans to join the party at Indianapolis.

Aboard the train are also a number of Mr. Lincoln's political associates. Two of them were his

Presidential campaign managers: Norman P. Judd, a close friend and prominent Chicago attorney; and Judge David Davis in whose Eighth Circuit Court the President-elect tried many cases. Others in the group include Jesse K. Dubois, state auditor; Ebenezer Peck, a Chicago politician; and Orville H. Browning, a former state senator from Quincy, Illinois.

The press is well represented by reporters from the *Chicago Tribune* and the *Illinois State Journal*. Henry Villard, the correspondent for the *New York Herald*, is aboard too. The dispatches to his newspaper will, by special arrangement, be picked up by the Associated Press and published all over the country.

Lucian Tilton, president of the Great Western Railway and a personal friend of Mr. Lincoln, heads the journey's operating personnel. As a precautionary measure, J. J. S. Wilson, superintendent of the Caton Telegraph Company, is also riding the train. He has with him a portable instrument that can be attached to the telegraph wires at any point in case there should be an emergency.

Some members of the official party will complete the trip. Others will journey only from Springfield to Indianapolis. And all along the way there will be constituents boarding the train to journey from one town to another, primarily to talk politics with Mr. Lincoln.

Early this morning the time card for the day was distributed to all employees of the Great Western

Railroad Company. It contains the following injunction:

> It is very important that this train should pass over the road in safety. . . . Red is the signal for danger, but any signal apparently intended to indicate alarm . . . must be regarded, the train stopped and the meaning of it ascertained. Carefulness is particularly enjoined.

At precisely five minutes before eight, Mr. Wood opens the door to the waiting room. He signals to the President-elect that the moment has come to leave. Mr. Lincoln bids good-bye to his wife and two younger sons, motioning Robert to follow him. Mr. Wood escorts his famous passenger through the crowd to the waiting train.

After mounting the steps to the rear platform, the President-elect turns to face the throng that has quickly surrounded the train. Suddenly he has the urge to say a few parting words to these people who have been his friends and neighbors for so many years. He removes his old stovepipe hat and holds up his right hand, then drops it on the platform railing as if to support himself.

The throng grows silent. Men take off their hats and stand bare-headed in the rain that has become a downpour. In a high thin voice, quavering with emotion, Mr. Lincoln says:

"My friends—no one, not in my situation, can appreciate my feeling of sadness at this parting.

"To this place, and the kindness of these people, I owe everything. Here I have lived a quarter of a century, and have passed from a young to an old man. Here my children have been born, and one is buried.

"I now leave, not knowing when, or whether ever, I may return, with a task before me greater than that which rested upon Washington.

"Without the assistance of that Divine Being, who ever attended him, I cannot succeed. With that assistance I cannot fail.

"Trusting in Him, who can go with me, and remain with you and be everywhere for good, let us confidently hope that all will yet be well.

"To His care commending you, as I hope in your prayers you will commend me, I bid you an affectionate farewell."

5 ABOARD THE PRESIDENTIAL SPECIAL
★ Monday, February 11, 1861 ★

The locomotive bell clangs noisily. Conductor Walt Whitney gives the signal, and the Presidential Special moves slowly away. Mr. Lincoln, his face moist with tears, waves good-bye and turns to enter the passenger coach. He is immediately surrounded by reporters. They want to know about the farewell speech he has just made. He had told them there would be no remarks; they have been caught unprepared. Will he please write down what he has said?

Mr. Lincoln explains that he had not intended to say anything; then somehow—seeing all the familiar faces—he couldn't help himself. It was just an impulse, but now he will set it down on paper. Accepting the pad handed to him by his secretary, the President-elect begins to write. The coach sways and jounces along the track; it is difficult to control his pencil. After completing three sentences, he hands the pad back to Nicolay and dictates the rest of the speech.

Because the journey has been well publicized, the people of Illinois know when to expect the train. There are groups clustered alongside the tracks in many places, waving flags and shouting lustily as the brightly colored cars roll past at thirty miles an hour.

Promptly at 9:24 A.M. the Special comes to a halt at the Decatur, Illinois, station. A cheering crowd surrounds the train. Mr. Lincoln is well known here and has many personal friends. He appears on the platform and attempts to say a few words. Unable to be heard above the din, he steps down and moves rapidly through the large gathering, shaking hands right and left. But the stop is only for a few moments. As the wheels begin to turn, he clambers aboard and waves at the receding faces.

Only a few miles beyond Decatur the Special brakes to an unscheduled halt. A stake-and-rider fence has been erected across the track. The train crew quickly removes the obstruction, and the pranksters loudly cheer. They have accomplished their purpose; Mr. Lincoln appears on the platform and waves to them.

On the outskirts of the next town, Bement, the tracks lead over a high trestle. There, as if to guard the Special, stands a uniformed soldier, rifle in hand. He presents arms as Mr. Lincoln's car passes.

It was in Bement that the President-elect met with Senator Stephen A. Douglas in 1858 to plan their famous debates. And the train now slows down so that Mr. Lincoln may salute the cheering spectators. Beyond the town limits, the Special gathers speed as it crosses the broad Illinois prairie land. The clouds are beginning to disappear; there are encouraging patches of blue in the sky.

At 10:50 A.M. the noisy twisting of the train's brakes signals the arrival at Tolono, a stop required by law because here the Great Western tracks cross those of the Illinois Central Railroad. Mr. Lincoln notes that a large group has assembled in a nearby grove of trees; he goes out to greet them. Mounting a bench provided for the occasion, he says:

> "My friends, I am leaving you on an errand of national importance, attended, as you are aware, with considerable difficulties. Let us believe, as some poet has expressed it, 'Behind the cloud the sun is still shining.' I bid you an affectionate farewell."

Since this stop is only for wood and water, Mr. Lincoln hurries back aboard. Again the train resumes its thirty-mile-an-hour pace across the flat prairie—through Philo, Sidney, Homer, Salina, Catlin, and Bryant, where waving throngs cheer the Special as it rolls by.

After the train crosses the Vermilion River, it comes to a stop in Danville. Many friends have gathered to greet the Special. Lamon accompanies Mr. Lincoln to the rear platform, but the engineer is four minutes behind schedule. There is time only for a few words. Briefly the President-elect remarks that Danville is one of the "dear places" in his memory, that if he has any blessings to give, he will "dispense the largest and roundest to my good old friends of Vermilion County." Both Lamon and the President-elect stand waving as the train departs.

The Special arrives at State Line at 12:38 P.M., eight minutes behind schedule. The Great Western line terminates here, connecting with the Toledo and Wabash Railroad. The village of six hundred people is divided by a public road with the round-house of one railroad in Illinois, of the other in Indiana. While the locomotives are being changed, the official party goes to the State Line Hotel for their noonday meal.

More than a thousand people are congregated in the public square. Some are wearing the buck-skins and coon caps of pioneers; others are smartly attired in plug hats and formal coats; but most are dressed in the faded workclothes of prairie farm-ers. Immediately after dinner, the Presidential party moves to the square where Captain Fred-erick Steele, chairman of the state legislature's welcoming committee, delivers a speech on behalf of the people of Indiana.

In response, Mr. Lincoln says:

"Gentlemen of Indiana; I am happy to meet you on this occasion, and enter again the state of my early life, and almost of maturity. I am under many obliga-tions to you for your kind reception, and to Indiana for the aid she rendered our cause, which, I think, a just one. . . ."

A sharp blast from the locomotive's whistle interrupts the speechmaking, and the official party hurries back to the Special.

Colonel Sumner has just come aboard. Instead of meeting the train in Indianapolis as he planned, he decided at the last minute to come to State Line. Because there have been disturbing rumors, arrangements have been made for a pilot engine to go down the track ahead of the Special. Officials of the Toledo and Wabash Railroad are taking no chances.

As the train steams off northeastward toward Lafayette, Mr. Lincoln stands alone on the rear platform watching his beloved Illinois prairies become a blur of land and sky. Reentering the coach, he hears Ward Hill Lamon strumming his banjo and singing "The Lament of the Irish Emigrant." Colonel Sumner is brushing his uniform while Colonel Ellsworth studies a manual of military tactics and portly Judge Davis snoozes after the hearty noon meal.

Shaking off the mood of melancholy that he experienced as he left Illinois, Mr. Lincoln joins the group of Indiana politicians who boarded the train at State Line. He appears to be stimulated by the delegation and the encouragement they provide for the task he is about to undertake.

A few minutes before half past two their conversation is interrupted by the crash of cannon.

Mr. Lincoln receives this noisy salute as the train grinds to a halt in the town of Lafayette on the banks of the Wabash River.

Hundreds are waiting when the President-elect emerges for a few brief remarks:

> "While some of us may differ in political opinions, still we are all united in one feeling for the Union. We all believe in the maintenance of the Union, of every star and stripe of the glorious flag, and permit me to express the sentiment that upon the union of the States, there shall be between us no difference. . . ."

The cheers are interrupted by the impatient engineer sounding the locomotive's whistle. In order to meet his strict time schedule, the engineer is anxious to be off. Within seconds the wheels begin to turn, and the train heads out southeast toward the center of the state. Moving along at a rapid speed, the engine necessarily consumes tremendous amounts of wood. A stop must be made at Thorntown to take on more fuel.

Here a noisy crowd calls out, "Speech! Speech!" Mr. Lincoln goes out to the rear platform and says that if he makes a speech at every stop, he will never get to Washington to be inaugurated. However, he will tell a story "if you promise not to let it out." The spectators shout, "No, no, we'll never tell."

"There was once a man who was to be nominated at a political convention," Mr. Lincoln begins, "and he hired a horse to journey there. The horse was so confoundedly slow, however . . . ."

Interrupting the story in midsentence, the train pulls away. There are shouts of "We'll never let *that* story out." The President-elect joins in the merriment and waves as the train disappears around the bend.

A short while later, the Special reaches Lebanon where a two-minute talk is scheduled. In the distance people can be seen running down the tracks. One of the party standing beside Mr. Lincoln jokes, "There come the folks from Thorntown to hear the rest of your story."

In a jovial mood the President-elect relates what happened at Thorntown and then tells the end of the story. The candidate, he says, arrived too late and found his opponent nominated and the convention adjourned. In returning the horse, he remarks that the animal was a good one but advises the stableman never to sell him to an undertaker.

Why not? the owner inquires. Because, says the candidate, if the horse were hitched to a hearse, Resurrection Day would come before he reached the cemetery. "And so," concludes Mr. Lincoln, "if my journey goes on at this slow rate, it will be Resurrection Day before I reach the capital."

Meanwhile, back in Springfield, Mrs. Lincoln has received a disturbing message from General Winfield Scott. The general believes that Mr. Lincoln will be much safer on this inaugural journey if he is surrounded by his family. That settles the matter for Mary Lincoln; she and Willie and Tad will go to Indianapolis at once. She summons

Burnett Forbes, William Wood's assistant who stayed behind to accompany her and the two younger boys.

Mr. Forbes makes arrangements for them to leave at 6:10 P.M. on the sleeper for Lafayette. There they will have to change railroads and catch the 7:20 A.M. train tomorrow for Indianapolis. It is scheduled to arrive just as the Presidential Special departs, but he promises they will make connections without any problem.

There's much excitement when Willie and Tad learn about the change in plans. They haven't liked the idea of being cooped up in the Chenery House. Lockwood Todd, Mrs. Lincoln's cousin, will be their escort—he's a great favorite with the boys. Also accompanying the family will be William Johnson, the Negro friend of the President-elect.

There's little time left in which to pack. As Mrs. Lincoln bustles through their hotel rooms, gathering up their possessions, she wonders why General Scott is so concerned about her husband's safety. Nevertheless, it's a good reason for joining him. Tomorrow will be Mr. Lincoln's birthday. His wife hopes he'll be happy to see his family.

6 ARRIVAL—AND A
MISSING ADDRESS
★ Monday, February 11, 1861 ★

While hasty preparations are being made in Springfield for Mrs. Lincoln's departure, the Presidential Special reaches Indianapolis at 5 P.M., precisely on schedule. Plans have been made for the party to detrain at West Washington Street rather than the Union Station, so the parade will have a longer route. Indiana's governor, Oliver P. Morton, is waiting here in his barouche. After greetings are exchanged, Mr. Lincoln listens to the governor's welcoming address.

In answer, the President-elect says that he is grateful for "this magnificent reception" and continues:

> "While I do not expect, upon this occasion, or on any occasion, till after I get to Washington, to attempt any lengthy speech, I will only say that to the salvation of this Union, there needs but one single thing—the hearts of a people like yours."

An outburst of applause greets his words. When the hubbub quiets down, Mr. Lincoln adds:

"My reliance will be placed upon you and the people
of the United States—and I wish you to remember
now and forever, that it is your business, and not
mine; that if the Union of these States, and the liberties of this people, shall be lost, it is but little to any
one man of fifty-two years of age, but a great deal
to the thirty millions of people who inhabit these
United States and to their posterity in all coming
time. It is your business to rise up and preserve the
Union and liberty, for yourselves, and not for me. . . ."

During the welcoming ceremony, a thirty-four
gun salute has been booming out across the city
at one-minute intervals. After Mr. Lincoln finishes,
he enters the governor's barouche where he shakes
hands with his host and with Mayor Samuel B.
Maxwell.

Behind the barouche are carriages for the Presidential party, legislators, and municipal author-
ities, followed by a procession of brass bands,
Zouaves, city firemen in their gaily decorated fire
engines, and several companies of Indiana guards-
men. When the entourage begins to move, there is
a sudden surge forward by the crowd hoping to
get a further sight of Mr. Lincoln. The line of
march is momentarily broken, and it is some minutes before order can be restored.

Down Washington Street, through the largest
numbers ever assembled in this state capital, the
parade inches along circling the business district
and coming to a halt at the Bates House. The President-elect rises and bows to the mass of people
who threaten to engulf him. Before leaving the

barouche, Mr. Lincoln leans over to the driver, Elijah Hedges, and compliments him on his handling of the matched team of four horses decorated with tiny American flags.

No sooner is the President-elect inside the hotel than the people on the streets begin calling for a speech. To oblige the twenty thousand massed here, he makes his way to a second-floor balcony and steps out into the chill twilight. Drawing the manuscript marked "For Indianapolis" from his coat pocket, Mr. Lincoln turns to the crowd. He understands the dilemma that has faced the Thirty-sixth Congress in reaching a decision about how to handle the states that have already seceded from the Union. Should these states be coerced into remaining as part of the United States? Should they be invaded by military force in order to protect federal property? The President-elect, determined not to evade the issue, presents it to the people as fairly as possible:

> "The words 'coercion' and 'invasion' are in great use about these days. . . . Would the marching of an army into South Carolina, for instance, without the consent of her people, and in hostility against them, be coercion or invasion? . . . If the Government, for instance, simply insists upon holding its own forts, or retaking those forts which belong to it, or the enforcement of the laws of the United States . . . would any or all of these things be coercion?"

The tall gaunt figure on the balcony then poses an even more serious question to all Americans:

"What is the particular sacredness of a State? . . .
I am speaking of that assumed right of a State, as a
primary principle, that the Constitution should rule
all that is less than itself, and ruin all that is bigger
than itself. But, I ask, wherein does consist that
right? . . . I am deciding nothing, but simply giving
something for you to reflect upon. . . . I thank you
again for this magnificent welcome. . . ."

Mr. Lincoln has chosen his words carefully for
this his first formal speech of the journey. It is
questionable, however, whether the many thousands gathered here have heard much of what he
has said. Nevertheless, the applause is deafening.
Now the President-elect reenters the hotel and
pushes his way through the corridors toward the
dining room. Nearly half an hour elapses before he
is served, and the meal is interrupted many times
by autograph hunters.

It had been planned that after dinner Mr. Lincoln
would hold a reception in his suite for members
of the Indiana legislature. That plan is abandoned,
however, because of the great numbers who insist
upon shaking hands with the President-elect.

In a room down the hall his private secretary, John Nicolay, is writing to his fiancée back in
Springfield. "The house is literally jammed full of
people," he confides. "Three or four ladies and as
many gentlemen have even invaded the room assigned to Mr. Lincoln; while outside the door I
hear the crowd grumbling and shouting in an almost frantic endeavor to get to another parlor at
the door of which Mr. Lincoln stands shaking

hands with the multitude. It is a severe ordeal for us, increased ten-fold for him."

Three thousand people file by the President-elect before he is able to end the ceremonial hand-shaking and retire to the suite reserved for him. Wryly he remarks that this has been harder work than "mauling rails."

Waiting for him is Mr. Lincoln's good friend Orville H. Browning. The former state senator planned to make the entire journey, but earlier this evening he wrote in his diary: "The trip to Indianapolis has been very pleasant, but is just about as much of that sort of thing as I want." He plans to return home to Quincy tomorrow and would like a few minutes alone with the President-elect.

Mr. Lincoln is pleased to see Senator Browning; he asks him to read the inaugural address. Please make suggestions concerning its contents, he adds. But where is the little black bag containing the precious document? What in the world has Robert done with the gripsack . . . and where is Robert himself? The President-elect is told that his son is "off with the boys." Find him at once, Mr. Lincoln orders, pacing the floor in agitation. What if some reporter has discovered the bag? Why, the in-augural address which he has guarded so carefully might be spread all over tomorrow morning's newspapers.

Almost an hour elapses before Robert appears, looking somewhat annoyed about being asked to return for anything so trivial as the location of a piece of luggage. Mr. Lincoln wants to know where the little black bag is. Robert explains that when he reached the hotel, no room had been provided for him. He merely handed the gripsack to the hotel clerk, and it had been stacked behind the counter with the other luggage.

Horrified, Mr. Lincoln throws open the door and elbows his way through the crowds to the lobby. A single stride of his long legs carries him flying over the clerk's desk, and he begins to search frantically through the mountain of luggage. The clerk watches in open-mouthed horror; bystanders crane their necks to see what is going on. Taking a small key from his pocket, Mr. Lincoln opens the first little black gripsack that resembles his own. Out falls a deck of cards, one dirty shirt, and some fresh paper collars. The unexpected contents are too much for the dignity of the President-elect; Mr. Lincoln joins in the laughter of the crowd.

Within minutes, however, the precious bag has been located, and he returns to his room, assuring Robert that from now on he will take charge of the gripsack. He pulls out a copy of the inaugural address and hands it to the senator. Will Browning be good enough to return it in the morning with any comments or suggestions?

It has been a long and strenuous day; the President-elect wastes no time in getting to bed. But sleep tonight is fitful. Thousands are roaming the streets below, shouting and laughing throughout the night. Unable to find accommodations, these Hoosiers are determined to have a part in the greatest political event the young frontier capital has ever witnessed.

7 ". . . IF YOU THE PEOPLE ARE BUT TRUE TO YOURSELVES . . ."
★ Tuesday, February 12, 1861 ★

Ever since dawn this morning, the crowds have been increasing outside Bates House. Shouts of "Speech! Speech!" and "We want Mr. Lincoln" have continued. Finally the President-elect appears on the balcony with his son Robert and Solomon T. Meredith, a legislator.

Excusing himself from delivering another address, Mr. Lincoln introduces his son to the crowd. This is Robert's first public appearance, and he merely waves, his father adding that Bob "hasn't got in the way of making speeches."

After breakfasting with Governor Morton at the mansion on Market Street, the President-elect goes to the state legislature and visits informally with its members. Then he returns to Bates House to meet the delegations that have arrived from Kentucky and Ohio.

A short distance down the hall, the Honorable Norman P. Judd is repacking his valise when there is a knock on the door. A Western Union messenger hands him a wire. Opening it, he reads:

> I have a message of importance for you—where can
> it reach you by special Messenger?
>
> (Signed) Allan Pinkerton.

The Illinois legislator has been well acquainted with the detective for a number of years. What can this possibly mean? And why the secrecy? He knows Pinkerton would not trouble him except on a matter of importance. Motioning to the messenger to wait, Judd whips out a scrap of paper and writes:

> Indianapolis 12 Feby 1861
>
> A Pinkerton
>
> At Columbus the thirteenth—Pittsburgh the fourteenth.
>
> N. B. Judd.

Back in Mr. Lincoln's hotel suite, the Illinois delegation has just arrived to bid farewell to their most famous citizen. Jesse Dubois manages to back Mr. Lincoln into a corner and hold his arms while Ebenezer Peck snips off a lock of the unruly black hair. They hug him affectionately and rush from the room, not wanting anyone to witness the depth of feeling they have for their longtime friend.

When Orville Browning arrives to say goodbye, Mr. Lincoln says he wants to have a private word with him, and the two men go into an adjoining bedroom. The President-elect is anxious to know what Senator Browning thinks of the inaugural address. It is well done and appropriate, says the senator, although there is one clause he doesn't like—there's too much implication of war. He suggests omitting the phrase where Mr. Lincoln declares that it will be his aim "to reclaim the public property and places which have fallen."

Because he has great respect for the senator's judgment, the President-elect strikes out the offending words. The two men return to the Illinois delegation, and Mr. Lincoln shakes hands all around. As the men leave, they ask Ward Lamon to accompany them for a few moments.

They all step into a room down the hall and lock the door. The burly Lamon is confronted by his old friends, who charge him with the importance of guarding the President-elect on the long journey ahead.

"We intrust the sacred life of Mr. Lincoln to your hands," says Jesse Dubois, "and if you don't protect it, never return to Illinois for we will murder you on sight." The threat is delivered in a jocular manner; nevertheless, these old friends share a common fear for the safety of the President-elect. The door is unlocked, and the Illinois delegation departs.

Returning to the Presidential suite, Lamon suggests it is time to leave for the railroad station. The horde of people clustered about the hotel entrance is so great that Lamon is forced to push his way through it first in order to get Mr. Lincoln out to Governor Morton's carriage. Immediately surrounded, the vehicle can move only a few feet at a time.

Meanwhile, Mrs. Lincoln, Willie, Tad, and their escorts have arrived at the railroad station. It has been a trying journey. Mrs. Lincoln was very disturbed. What if their train were delayed? She kept insisting the conductor wire ahead at various intervals to make certain they would not be left behind. Under the guidance of Burnett Forbes, the little group makes its way to the rear car of the Presidential Special where they will wait for the arrival of Mr. Lincoln.

The Union Station this morning is overflowing. Seven railroads run into the capital, and the various lines have been giving half-fare excursion rates for this special occasion. Thousands of Hoosiers have come to Indianapolis to see and cheer the President-elect.

The Indianapolis and Cincinnati Railroad has added three freshly varnished passenger cars to the Special. The entire train is decorated with tricolor bunting and American flags; the front of the new locomotive, the *Samuel Wiggins*, is covered with portraits of past American Presidents as well as of the President-elect, while the sides are draped with flags and evergreen branches. On the platform railing is a huge garland of red, white, and blue, with a large gilded American eagle in the center.

It is with considerable difficulty that Ward Lamon shoves through the mass of spectators to clear a path for the Presidential party. Mr. Lincoln accepts the buffeting good-naturedly and mounts the rear platform to wave to the thousands sur-

rounding the train. Delegations from adjoining
states have been asked to sit in the first two
coaches, while members of the Presidential party
go into the third coach, the last one being reserved
for Mr. Lincoln and his family.

Promptly at eleven o'clock the Special begins
moving, and the President-elect bows to the shouting mob. Through the switching yards, along the
drab industrial area, and thence to the outlying
suburbs, the train creeps along. Every half mile
are stationed armed sentinels, who wave American flags to signal that all is well.

When the Special reaches the open countryside,
Mr. Lincoln turns and enters the rear coach. Willie
and Tad, who have been waiting impatiently for
this moment, pounce on their father in high glee.
He is both surprised and pleased to see his wife
and two younger sons. Mrs. Lincoln's first words
are to wish her husband a happy birthday, an
event he has momentarily forgotten in the day's
excitement. Enfolding the two boys in his arms,
Mr. Lincoln bends over to kiss his wife, his eyes
moist with emotion. She looks radiant, he tells her
affectionately.

Within a few moments the boys scamper off to
explore the rest of the train, and Mr. Lincoln introduces his wife to the delegations from Kentucky
and Ohio. This is a proud and happy time for him.

There is a two-minute stop at Shelbyville and
another at Greensburg—only long enough for the
President-elect to wave from the rear platform.

Reentering the car, he takes time to look over the pile of newspapers which have been delivered earlier. He is anxious to know how his speech of last night has been received.

The *Cleveland Leader* reports that "Mr. Lincoln has acquitted himself not only creditably but nobly." And the *Chicago Tribune* says: "This little speech has electrified the true Republicans and has given the fishy ones 'fever and ague.'" But the *Charleston* (South Carolina) *Mercury* derides the address, sneering that the President-elect is serving up "a dish of fiddle-faddle." Southerners are not alarmed, the editorial writer continues, because they know he is "a weak compound of blockhead and blackguard."

Mr. Lincoln is not surprised that the Southern newspapers are trying to degrade him. Nevertheless, one of the main reasons for this long journey is to persuade the citizenry that the nation must be united at all costs.

The last stop in Indiana is Lawrenceburg. Just across the river lies the slaveholding state of Kentucky. Here at the gaily festooned depot of the Indianapolis and Cincinnati Railroad, Mr. Lincoln greets the crowd:

> "My fellow-countrymen, you call upon me for a speech; I have none to give to you, and have not sufficient time to devote to it if I had. I suppose you are all Union men here."

There are cries of "Right, Right!"

> "And I suppose that you are in favor of doing full

justice to all, whether on that side of the river [pointing to the Kentucky shore], or on your own."

Lusty cheers and cries of "We are, we are," reach Mr. Lincoln's ears.

"If the politicians and leaders of parties were as true as the PEOPLE, there would be little fear that the peace of the country would be disturbed. I have been selected to fill an important office for a brief period, and am now, in your eyes, invested with an influence that will soon pass away; but should my administration prove to be a very wicked one, or what is more probable, a very foolish one, if you, the PEOPLE, are but true to yourselves and to the Constitution, there is but little harm I can do, thank God!"

As soon as Mr. Lincoln finishes speaking, the people surge forward to shake his hand. But the train pulls rapidly away, and he can only wave at the receding crowd.

It is exactly 12:20 P.M. when Norman Judd's wire reaches the Chicago office of the Pinkerton Detective Agency. Mr. Bangs, the superintendent in charge, wastes no time in summoning the special messenger who will deliver the letter from Allan Pinkerton. He wires:

W. H. Scott
Lafayette, Ind.
J— says will be at Columbus Thirteenth—Pittsburgh Fourteenth—form your own estimate by inquiring at Indianapolis.

G. H. Bangs

At about this same time the Presidential Special is approaching North Bend, just across the Ohio line; Mr. Lincoln hurries to the rear platform. He knows that William Henry Harrison, ninth President of the United States, is buried here, and wants to pay his respects. Members of the Harrison family have gathered at the gravesite, only a short distance from the railroad tracks. As the train slows down and passes the cemetery, Mr. Lincoln lifts off his stovepipe hat and stands with his head bowed.

Since early morning great numbers of people have been gathering in Cincinnati to welcome Mr. Lincoln. When the train pulls into the city, police and military personnel find it necessary to clear the tracks of spectators before the Special can proceed. As a result, it is a few minutes after the scheduled hour of three o'clock when the cars come to a halt in the Ohio and Mississippi Railroad depot at the foot of Fifth Street.

The President-elect is welcomed by Mayor Richard M. Bishop, the crowd roaring approval. Mr. Lincoln climbs into the open carriage and shakes hands with two gentlemen from Kentucky who, together with the mayor, will accompany him.

Cincinnati has prepared well for the arrival. Brass bands, fife-and-drum corps, LaFayette Guards, Zouaves, and a regiment of Washington Dragoons head the lengthy procession as it begins an orderly march through the city. The open carriage, decorated with bunting and drawn by six white horses, is surrounded by a detachment of police.

The elaborate decorations on the parade route do not go unnoticed by the President-elect. He sees the colorful banners stretched across the streets, the windows adorned with portraits of Washington and Lincoln encircled by evergreens. On one house is a mammoth sign reading: WELCOME TO THE PRESIDENT OF THIRTY-FOUR STATES; on another, a large flag with one word—UNION— spelled out below it.

As the procession winds through the downtown streets of Cincinnati, Mr. Lincoln often rises from his seat and bows. On Vine Street at the Banner Ward House there are thirty little girls standing on tables that line the street. The parade stops while they sing "The Star-Spangled Banner." One of the youngsters is carried over to the carriage and presents Mr. Lincoln with a single rose, which he accepts and, in turn, kisses the tot on both cheeks.

It is almost five thirty when the procession arrives in front of the Burnet House at Third and Vine. The President-elect is escorted inside, but reappears almost immediately on the second-floor balcony with Mayor Bishop. He raises his hand to silence the wildly cheering throng. After an introduction by the mayor, Mr. Lincoln begins:

"Twenty-four hours ago at the capital of Indiana, I

said to myself I have never seen so many people assembled together in winter weather. I am no longer able to say that. . . .

"My friends, I am entirely overwhelmed by the magnificence of the reception which has been given, I will not say to me, but to the President-elect of the United States of America. Most heartily do I thank you, one and all for it."

Thunderous applause greets these words. When the people quiet down, Mr. Lincoln goes on to say that all political parties are represented here, and he hopes that for centuries to come "under the free institutions of America," there will be such good-will toward every elected President. To allay the fears of all Southerners, he gestures toward the slaveholding state of Kentucky, lying just across the Ohio River.

"We mean to treat you, as near as we possibly can, as Washington, Jefferson, and Madison treated you . . . that under the Providence of God, who has never deserted us, that we shall again be brethren, forgetting all parties, ignoring all parties. My friends, I now bid you farewell."

After supper there is a reception in the main dining room. For more than two hours, Mr. Lincoln stands on a small platform and shakes hands with all who pour into the room. Seeing their honored guest begin to show signs of fatigue, Mayor Bishop suggests that Mr. Lincoln mount a nearby chair and bid his well-wishers good night.

The President-elect accepts the idea gratefully

and within moments a cordon of police and military officers forms to conduct him through the well-guarded corridors to his suite. The arrangements committee in Cincinnati has planned well. There has been no pushing, no shoving; the crowds have been enthusiastic but orderly.

When Mr. Lincoln enters the suite, he finds one more task to complete before retiring. Back in Springfield there had been a nightly ritual with his youngest son, Tad. The fretful little boy, refusing all entreaties from his mother, is now dozing in a chair, waiting for his father to put him to bed. Lovingly the President-elect gathers up the child in his arms and carries him into an adjoining bedroom. Only half-awake, Tad smiles at his father as Mr. Lincoln undresses him, pulling the night shirt over the child's head and gently placing him beside his sleeping brother.

Outside, the crowds have dispersed. Quiet pervades the streets of Cincinnati as this second day of the inaugural journey ends.

8 CONSTERNATION IN TWO CAPITALS
★ Wednesday, February 13, 1861 ★

Unable to sleep, the President-elect is up by 6:15 A.M. on this the third day of the inaugural journey. He cannot seem to shake off his feeling of dark foreboding. At noon today in Washington, D.C., the electoral votes will be counted in the presence of both houses of Congress, as provided in the Constitution.

There has been much talk about secessionist plots to take over the federal government. Early last January Senator William H. Seward of New York had become very concerned. Seward had been Mr. Lincoln's leading rival for the Republican Presidential nomination, but once the party had made its choice, the senator turned his political efforts toward saving the Union. He sent a letter to Mr. Lincoln, warning him of these secessionist plots.

In reply, the President-elect wrote: "It seems to me the inauguration is not the most dangerous point for us. Our adversaries have us more clearly at a disadvantage . . . when the votes shall be officially counted. If the two Houses refuse to meet at all, or meet without a quorum of each, where shall we be?" Despite his deep concern about the outcome of today's congressional session, Mr. Lincoln presents a cheerful appearance as he bids good-bye to the Indiana delegation after breakfast.

Upstairs, Norman Judd is still packing when there is a sharp rap on his door. The caller identifies himself as W. H. Scott, special messenger from the Pinkerton Detective Agency. Mr. Judd invites the man into his room and accepts the envelope offered him. Glancing at its contents, he does his best to conceal the horror that sweeps over him. A plot to assassinate the President-elect? It isn't possible. Yet he knows that Pinkerton is not an alarmist, that he must have good evidence to have written such a thing.

Judd then asks if the messenger has come from Chicago, explaining that he answered Pinkerton's wire yesterday by saying he could be reached in Columbus today. Scott explains that when he left Chicago last night, the wire had not yet been received, but he hoped to be able to deliver the letter this morning before the departure of the Special.

The legislator is very grateful and says so; he speaks warmly of Pinkerton, adding, "We trained in the same school together." Cautioning that the information must be kept "strictly confidential,"

Scott says good-bye, and Judd finishes packing, his mind in a turmoil. It's almost eight thirty—the carriages will be leaving for the trip to the Little Miami Railroad depot. He hurries out to join the other members of the Presidential party.

Today one hundred persons will ride in the three coaches that comprise the special train. Press and railroad personnel are to be in the first car; the second coach will carry local committees and staff members, while the rear car is reserved for Mr. Lincoln and his family. Already aboard is Anson Stager, superintendent for Western Union. He carries with him a portable instrument like the one J. J. S. Wilson had when the Special left Springfield. If any emergency arises, the instrument can be used for instant contact by wireless.

A pilot engine will again precede the Special to Ohio's state capital. Last night there were reports that an attempt had been made to derail the train near State Line, Indiana, and this morning some-one started the story that a grenade was discovered in one of the coaches. Colonel Lamon has tried to dispel fear by saying this is only newspaper talk. Nevertheless, the Little Miami Railroad officials are taking no chances.

The sun is shining; the temperature is mild as the wheels of the Special begin turning promptly at 9 A.M. The train chugs into the Ohio country-side, making stops at Milford, Loveland, and Mor-row. Between towns Mr. Lincoln chats amiably with the newsmen aboard. He sounds as if he had a heavy cold this morning; he is hoarse from the speechmaking of the previous two days but laughingly says his husky voice is merely a hazard of his new job.

The reporters try to steer the conversation toward politics; the President-elect, however, skillfully avoids any definite statement. When asked about the secessionist demands on the federal government, Mr. Lincoln says it reminds him of a dispute several years ago between his younger sons. Willie had a toy that Tad wanted. A great clamor arose, both boys asserting their rights. To make peace, Willie was told to give the toy to Tad in order to quiet his screams. "No, sir," was Willie's staunch answer, "I must have it to quiet myself."

While the train continues its thirty-mile-an-hour rate along the Little Miami's track, excitement is running high in Washington, D.C. Rumor has it that Southern secessionists plan to pack the gallery seats of the House chamber today, and when the counting of the electoral votes begins, they will cause a riot and seize the building, thus preventing Abraham Lincoln from being declared President.

General Winfield Scott, commander of the Army, heard the rumor some time ago and said "that any man who attempted to . . . interfere with the lawful count of the electoral vote . . . should be lashed to the muzzle of a twelve-pounder and fired out of the window of the Capitol. I would

manure the hills of Arlington with the fragments of his body." True to his word, General Scott has posted armed guards at all entrances to the Capitol. A full regiment of soldiers, dressed in civilian clothes, has been issued passes for the gallery. They are positioned to act in the event of any disturbance. Guns and ammunition have been stacked in two committee rooms adjoining the House chamber.

As early as eight o'clock this morning, gangs of hecklers have been heading up Pennsylvania Avenue to the Capitol. They are stopped at every doorway. No one may enter except members of the House and Senate and those with a written ticket of admission signed by the Speaker of the House or the Vice-President. Many who are refused admittance hurl resentful epithets at the guards.

At twenty minutes before twelve, the door-keeper of the House announces the arrival of the Senate. Led by the Vice-President, John C. Breckenridge, the members enter. Taking his seat as presiding officer, the Vice-President announces that in accordance with the Constitution it is now his duty to open the certificates of election. He hands the papers to the two tellers, appointed by the House and Senate.

The counting begins, state by state. A ripple of laughter sweeps through the gallery of spectators as the votes of seceded South Carolina are cast for John C. Breckenridge. Outside the building the guards are having trouble controlling the ever increasing numbers of people. Pennsylvania Avenue is filled with angry mobs. When fighting breaks out, the police move in and seize the ringleaders, placing them under arrest. In contrast to this uproar, all is peaceful in the House chamber. The counting continues.

Meanwhile, the Special is rolling across Ohio. At Zenia the group will detrain for dinner. Arriving there shortly before one o'clock, Mr. Wood hurries into the dining room to make sure that everything is ready. He is horrified. The meal prepared for the Presidential party has already been consumed by those awaiting the train's arrival. He is told that an unruly group stormed the dining room demanding food—not a morsel remains. There is nothing to do but to continue the journey.

As the train pulls into London, Mr. Lincoln looks out the window and sees a group of brightly uniformed musicians waiting to perform. He makes his appearance, waves to the crowd, and says, "I perceive a band of music present, and while the iron horse stops to water himself, I would prefer they should discourse in their more eloquent music than I am capable of." The people laugh, and the proud musicians begin their noisy serenade, continuing until after the Special is out of sight.

It is nearly two o'clock when the train slows down on the outskirts of Columbus. In the rear coach Senator James Monroe, chairman of the legislative reception committee, approaches and explains that he is supposed to take Mr. Lincoln's arm as he escorts him from the train to the carriage now awaiting. The President-elect rises. The senator, looking at the six-foot-four figure beside him, adds, "Although it is etiquette you should take 'my' arm, your stature makes that awkward, so we had better reverse the order."

Mr. Lincoln accepts the senator's suggestion and chuckles. "As for etiquette, I never was overburdened with it." Once the train stops, the two men walk side by side to the carriage. The procession threads its way through the densely packed crowds up High Street to the state capitol.

There another large throng is waiting on the capitol steps. In answer to shouts of "Speech, speech," Governor Dennison promises that the President-elect will have a few words to say to them later. Inside the building, both houses of the legislature have assembled to welcome their honored guest. After an introduction by Lieutenant Governor Robert C. Kirk, Mr. Lincoln rises and says:

"It is true ... that very great responsibility rests upon me in the position to which the votes of the American people have called me. ... There has fallen upon me a task such as did not rest even upon the Father of his country, and so feeling I cannot but turn and look for the support without which it will be impossible for me to perform that great task. I turn, then, and look to the American people and to that God who has never forsaken them. ..."

The applause is heartening, but Mr. Lincoln cannot help worrying about what is happening this afternoon in another legislative session. Has there been trouble in the national capital, as so many have warned there would be?

Governor Dennison now escorts his guest out to the capitol steps where the crowd has waited patiently for the promised "few words." Mr. Lincoln thanks them for the kind reception and continues speaking in a more serious vein:

"I am doubly thankful that you have appeared here to give me this greeting. It is not much to me, for I shall very soon pass away from you; but we have a large country and a large future before us, and the manifestations of good-will toward the government, and affection for the Union which you may exhibit are of immense value to you and to your posterity forever. ..."

After Mr. Lincoln has finished, the governor announces there will be a public reception in the capitol rotunda. The line, he says, should form up near the south entrance and pass by the north stairway in an orderly manner. Once the doors are opened, however, there is a frantic rush. A jostling pushing crowd swarms into the building, and only through the efforts of several police is the President-elect saved from being injured by the physical pressure of the enthusiastic mob. He shakes hands rapidly—to the right, to the left, both hands at once, and sometimes reaches out to grasp a hand extended above the heads of those who are nearest him.

Noting that Mr. Lincoln looks very tired, the governor calls a halt to the wild reception and suggests they retire to his private office. When the President-elect enters the room, Western Union Superintendent Stager hands him a dispatch just in from Washington. Eagerly the men gathered in the office watch his face as Mr. Lincoln reads silently:

The votes were counted peaceably. You are elected.

Looking up, he sees everyone watching him. Turning to his host, he says: "What a beautiful building you have here, Governor Dennison." The anxious expressions on the faces of his friends turn to smiles. It is quite evident there has been no crisis in the nation's capital.

Ohio's festivities for the famous visitor are not yet over. The Lincoln family are house guests of the governor, and tonight there is a reception at the executive mansion, followed by a military ball given by the governor's guards.

While the President-elect is leading the grand promenade in Deshler Hall, the *New York Herald* correspondent, Henry Villard, is writing the daily dispatch for his newspaper:

> No one can see Mr. Lincoln without recognizing in him a man of immense power and force of character and natural talent. He seems so sincere, so conscientious, so earnest, so simple-hearted that one cannot help liking him. . . . With a great self-possession and self-control, with the intimate knowledge of politics and politicians, and with the uncommon homespun common sense which his friends claim for him, Lincoln seems a man to act and decide for himself, and not be entrapped. He seems tremendously rough, and tremendously honest.

9 DELAYED BY A DERAILMENT
⋆ Thursday, February 14, 1861 ⋆

The governor's private barouche and several state carriages line up outside the executive mansion early this morning. Precisely at seven o'clock Mr. Lincoln and his family appear, accompanied by Governor Dennison and his reception committee. They drive off to the Columbus depot in orderly fashion, unimpeded by throngs of spectators. In spite of the rain on this fourth day of the journey, several hundred people have gathered at the station to bid farewell to Ohio's visitor.

Today the Presidential Special consists of the locomotive—*Washington City*—the baggage car, and two coaches. Past experience has proved that the more coaches there are, the more people want to ride on the Special. Superintendent Wood has issued an order that only those he approves are acceptable. In his official capacity, he feels it necessary to protect Mr. Lincoln in every way possible.

Once the train leaves the Columbus station, Mr. and Mrs. Lincoln enjoy conversing with the members of the escorting committee who are to ride with them as far as Pittsburgh. In the forward car the young people gather to listen to Colonel Lamon strum his banjo—a pleasant diversion on this dreary morning. He sings the novelty hit "Sparkin' on a Sunday," and everyone joins in when he begins "Dixey's Land."

There are two-minute stops at Newark, Frazeyburg, Dresden, Cochocton, Newcomerstown, and Uhrichsville where the President-elect is warmly greeted despite the rain. Choruses, bands, and volleys of artillery prove their enthusiasm. Mr. Lincoln is astonished at the number of people who braved the foul weather merely to hear him say a few words.

A noontime stopover is made at Cadiz Junction; the Presidential party is ushered to nearby Parks House for dinner. It is a sumptuous meal, one of the best thus far on the journey. Afterward, Mr. Lincoln appears on the platform to tell the assembled gathering that he cannot make a speech; he is "too full of utterance." Then he adds that if only there were time, "we would organize the train, and pass a vote of thanks to the people of Harrison County for the excellent dinner we have received."

Amid shouts of laughter and applause, the train heads out of town. During a lull in the conversation Mr. Lincoln takes the opportunity to look over some newspapers that have been placed in the rear coach.

The *Ohio State Journal* has noted that yesterday the President-elect "looked somewhat worn with travel and the fatigues of popularity," but also "something in his manner, even more than in his words, told how deeply he was affected by the enthusiasm of the people." The reporter's words are gratifying, though Mr. Lincoln knows that despite the complimentary remarks, there are many editorial writers who will twist his words and try to deride him.

Reaching for the *Baltimore Sun,* he reads:

> We begin to wonder what manner of man he is. There is that about his speechification which, if it were not for the gravity of the occasion, would be ludicrous to the destruction of buttons. Indeed we heard his Columbus speech read yesterday amidst irresistible bursts of laughter. And it was suggested, in the language of Dr. Holmes, that Mr. Lincoln is a man who ought never to be as funny as he can. We begin to realize his qualifications as a barroom "Phunny Phellow."

By the time the Special reaches Steubenville, the low-hanging dark clouds have broken, and the sun suddenly appears—a good omen, the passengers tell each other. Cannon boom out, and a chorus sings "The Red, White, and Blue" as the President-elect is taken to a carpeted stage that has been erected beside the tracks. Today the Virginians, just across the river, appear to have forgotten their differences. They have joined the Ohioans—some ten thousand in all—to greet Mr. Lincoln.

In response to Judge W. R. Lody's welcome, the

President-elect looks across the broad Ohio River toward the gently rolling hills of Virginia and says he believes devotion to the Constitution is equally great on both sides. Then he continues:

> "The question is, as to what the Constitution means— 'What are the rights under the Constitution?' . . . To decide that, who shall be the judge? Can you think of any other, than the voice of the people . . . ?
>
> "Though the majority may be wrong, and I will not undertake to say that they were not wrong in electing me, yet we must adhere to the principle that the majority shall rule. By your Constitution you have another chance in four years. No great harm can be done by us in that time. . . . If anything goes wrong, however, and you find you have made a mistake, elect a better man next time. There are plenty of them."

Rolling out of Steubenville at half past two, the train winds northward along the Ohio River. The next stop is Wellsville, where after the usual greetings an old man pushes his way forward to the edge of the train platform.

"God bless ye, Mister Lincoln!" he says. "I didn't vote for ye, but I sure would like to shake yer paw."

The President-elect smilingly extends his hand and asks for whom the old gentleman voted.

"Mister Dooglas" is the reply. The crowd laughs heartily.

"Well, my friend," says Mr. Lincoln, "if you and the other friends of Mr. Douglas will help me keep the ship of state afloat for the next four years, then

Mr. Douglas will have another chance. But if we allow it to go to pieces, Mr. Douglas will never get to be President."

Wild applause splits the air; the people stamp and cheer as the train moves out of the Wellsville station, Mr. Lincoln bowing from the rear platform.

There is a long finger of land that reaches northward from Virginia, separating Ohio from Pennsylvania. It is slaveholding territory, and the occupants of the Special are somewhat uneasy while the train is passing through this section. The tension lifts, however, as soon as they cross the Pennsylvania border—they are back on loyal Northern soil.

The first stop in Pennsylvania is at Rochester. Though hoarse from having used his voice so much today, Mr. Lincoln does not want to disappoint the flag-waving crowd. Thanking them for this expression of their good wishes, he says that as they know he is now on his way to Washington and about the fourth of March he will speak to all who choose to hear him.

A heckling voice from the back of the crowd shouts, "What will you do with the secessionists then?"

A sudden sadness appears in the eyes of the President-elect. He turns toward the direction of the voice, answering, "My friend, that is a matter which I have under very grave consideration."

Pittsburgh is still some miles away when the

train begins slowing down. At first no one notices, but as the engineer eases up on the throttle, they begin to wonder. The cars brake to a sudden stop near Freedom, Pennsylvania, and presently the passengers are told that a freight train has been derailed up ahead. The Special can go no farther until the tracks are cleared. There is speculation as to the cause. Have the heavy rains contributed to the accident? Has someone deliberately loosened the rails? Mr. Lincoln pays no attention to the sinister rumors and continues to chat with his associates.

Word spreads quickly through the town of Freedom that the Presidential Special has made an unscheduled stop. Soon people come streaming from every direction and surround the train. Calls for Mr. Lincoln bring him outside.

Once the President-elect has finished his greeting, a coal miner yells, "Abe, you say you're the tallest man in the United States, but I don't believe you're any taller than I am."

Mr. Lincoln breaks into a hearty laugh. "Come up here and let's measure."

The dusty miner in his workclothes edges forward, climbs over the platform railing, and stands back to back with the President-elect. The two men are so near the same height that Mr. Lincoln asks Colonel Ellsworth to referee. The stubby little colonel clambers up on top of the railing, runs his hands over the tops of the two heads, and calls out that they are the same height. There are shouts

of approval as the two men grin at each other and shake hands.

This incident, like others thus far, contributes to the American people's understanding of the friendly Illinoisan whom they have elected to be their President. Mr. Lincoln was little known outside his own state last November. But the rear-platform talks, the public receptions, the handshaking, the occasional incidents all are ways of winning the national confidence.

When the tracks are finally cleared, the Special travels the last miles into Pittsburgh, arriving at seven o'clock, two hours late. The rain is now coming down in torrents. An extensive parade through the city had been planned, but it has had to be canceled because of the weather. Nevertheless, a band of well-wishers has come to see the President-elect.

Mr. Lincoln and his party duck into waiting carriages and begin the drive to the Monongahela House. During the rain-soaked procession, a frantic moment for Colonel Lamon occurs. A horse belonging to one of the cavalry escorts becomes frightened and rears, its front hoofs coming perilously close to the carriage in which Mr. Lincoln is seated. He takes no notice of the narrow escape and continues to talk with his host.

In spite of the rain, excitement runs high in this Pennsylvania city. The wet weather has not discouraged hundreds of people from congregating in front of the hotel. When the carriage arrives,

Mr. Lincoln gets out and looks over the sea of umbrellas.

> "Fellow citizens, we had an accident upon the road today, and were delayed till this late hour. . . . I could not help thinking, my friends, as I traveled in the rain through your crowded streets, on my way here, that if all that people were in favor of the Union, it can certainly be in no great danger—it will be preserved."

Thanking them for their cordial reception, he promises to speak at greater length tomorrow morning, "when we may hope for more favorable weather."

10 "... KEEP COOL ..."
★ Friday, February 15, 1861 ★

Although torrential rain is still falling on the city
this morning, thousands stand huddled under umbrellas outside the Monongahela House. Evidently
the storm has failed to deter anyone; newsmen report that it's the largest crowd ever assembled in
Pittsburgh's history.

Mr. Lincoln is heartened by such a display of
loyalty as he appears on the balcony to make the
speech he promised last night. He thanks the people for their "flattering reception" and launches
into a discussion of the crisis confronting the nation. "The condition of the country," he says, "is
an extraordinary one, and fills the mind of every
patriot with anxiety and solicitude...."

Continuing the same theme, Mr. Lincoln coun-
sels:

> "My advice, then, under such circumstances is to keep
> cool. If the great American people will only keep
> their temper, on both sides of the line, the troubles
> will come to an end, and the question which now dis-

tracts the country will be settled just as surely as all other difficulties of like character which have originated in this government have been adjusted . . . and this great nation shall continue to prosper as heretofore."

As soon as the President-elect finishes speaking, he is informed it is time to leave for Cleveland. He asks for a few extra moments. Leonard Swett, elector-at-large from Illinois, has been detained here at the hotel for several weeks because of illness; Mr. Lincoln wishes to have a few words with his good friend.

It is almost half past nine before the Presidential party leaves the Monongahela House. Cheering mobs slow the line of carriages as the horses pick their way through the muddy streets. The special train has not yet arrived when the procession reaches the depot, and the crowd follows Mr. Lincoln inside. There is much shoving and pushing, though the President-elect is more amused than annoyed by the jostling mob.

Over the heads of the people, one determined father passes his young son into the outstretched arms of the tall man from Illinois. The little boy receives a hearty kiss on the cheek. Three attractive young women elbow their way up to Mr. Lincoln and receive the same greeting. But when younger members of the Presidential party try to kiss the girls, they are firmly repulsed. Mr. Lincoln joins in the laughter that results from this boldness.

The Special with its two coaches and baggage car has now pulled into position, and the Presidential party is escorted out to the waiting train amid resounding cheers. Arrangements have been made to give Robert a unique privilege this morning; instead of taking his customary place in the rear coach with the rest of the family, he climbs into the cab of the locomotive *Comet*. Engineer Williamson has promised that Robert will be his assistant today. Under expert direction, the young man can manage the controls. A battery of guns punctuates Pittsburgh's noisy farewell as the train begins picking up momentum.

Once out of the city, Mr. Lincoln turns to the stack of newspapers beside his chair. How are the reporters viewing his activities? Despite the acid remarks of the pro-Southern periodicals, there is satisfaction in the appraisal of the *Pittsburgh Gazette*: "The impression he made upon our citizens generally, by his personal bearing and public remarks, was highly favorable; while his courteous and friendly manner captivated all. . . ." A slow smile spreads across the deeply lined face of the President-elect as he reads the *Chicago Tribune's* summary: "Let the people shout! This time their hero is an honest man!"

Retracing yesterday's journey through Rochester, Pennsylvania, the train again stops at Wellsville, Ohio—a railroad division point. While the locomotive is being changed, Mr. Lincoln strides to the rear platform for a breath of air and tells the crowd he will not make a speech; he did that yesterday in this very same spot.

At that moment an old man pushes forward and hands him a highly polished red apple. From the edge of the crowd comes the shrill voice of a small boy. "Say, Mr. Lincoln," he yells, "that man is running for postmaster!" The President-elect is obviously amused, and the audience breaks into laughter.

At the next stops—Salineville and Bayard, Ohio—he merely appears on the platform and waves. Mr. Lincoln is now so hoarse that he feels he must save his voice for those speeches already scheduled. Out in the countryside once more, conversation is kept to a minimum. The President-elect makes a few penciled notes but is more interested in the game that Willie and Tad are playing on the floor of the coach.

When the train halts at Alliance, Ohio, shortly after the noon hour, the Presidential party is taken to Sourbeck's Hotel for a dinner given by the railroad's president, John N. McCullough. Outside the hostelry, a company of Canton Zouaves stands guard; a band entertains with patriotic tunes. One disturbing incident occurs, however. An artillery salute is fired too close to the building. Windows are smashed; Mrs. Lincoln is sprayed with flying glass. It is momentarily alarming, but fortunately no one is hurt.

The afternoon schedule calls for stops at Hudson and Ravenna, before the arrival in Cleveland. The

railroad has run excursions from Akron and
Cuyahoga Falls to see the President-elect, and
there is a loud roar from the crowd as the train
pulls into Hudson. Some six thousand people have
gathered here. In spite of his husky throat, Mr.
Lincoln manages to rasp out a greeting, although
the train is late and the engineer is anxious to leave.
Another huge crowd is waiting at Ravenna, causing the reporter for the *Cleveland Herald* to write
that the journey has been a "continuous succession of ovations."

It is almost dusk when the Special slows down
for the Euclid Street depot, two miles from the
center of Cleveland. Thousands of citizens—on
horseback, in carriages, and on foot—await the
train's arrival. Fire companies with brightly decorated engines, a company of Cleveland Grays who
will act as a military escort, omnibuses filled
with workmen from local factories—all are ready
to parade into town.

As the train comes to a halt, an artillery company fires the Presidential salute. Mr. Lincoln
emerges, and thousands acclaim his arrival.
Robert, climbing down from the locomotive cab,
is met by a group of Young Republicans. They
hand him the reins of a handsome horse and sug-
gest that he ride directly behind the Presidential
carriage.

A brisk wind whips the hundreds of flags flying
along Euclid Street as the parade moves slowly

through the massed thousands. Though exhausted by the rigors of a long day, the President-elect stands in the open carriage and bows to the shouting spectators along the parade route.

It is half past five when the procession draws up in front of the Weddell House at Superior and Banks streets. Colonel Lamon jumps out to clear a pathway for Mr. Lincoln. The party hastens inside, but within minutes the President-elect reappears on a platform, built out from the second-floor balcony of the hotel.

There are welcoming speeches by J. E. Master, president of the city council, and Judge Sherlock J. Andrews. In response Mr. Lincoln says:

> "We have been marching about two miles through snow, rain and deep mud. The large numbers that have turned out under these circumstances testify that you are in earnest about something or other. But do I think so meanly of you as to suppose that that earnestness is about me personally? I would be doing you injustice to suppose you did. You have assembled to testify your respect to the Union, the Constitution and the laws, and here let me say that it is with you, the people, to advance the great cause of the Union and the Constitution, and not with any one man. It rests with you alone. . . ."

He closes his speech by thanking the people for the devotion they have displayed to the cause of the Union. Because Mr. Lincoln is so hoarse, it is very possible that only the few people closest to the balcony can hear what he says. The applause is wild, however; cheers echo through the streets as he turns and reenters the hotel for a short rest before the evening's festivities.

After dinner, there is a reception to honor the President-elect, while Mrs. Lincoln holds her own levee. Mr. Lincoln stands in line and shakes hands until shortly after ten o'clock, when he retires to his suite to be interviewed by the editor of the *Cleveland Plain Dealer.*

At that very hour some three hundred and fifty miles away in Baltimore, Allan Pinkerton is writing up his daily report of activities. During the past few days he has made it a point to express contempt for the incoming President; he has even contributed a handsome sum of money to the secessionist cause. Through a Mr. Luckett, one of the leaders of the Maryland secessionists, he has wangled an introduction to the barber at Barnum's Hotel, Cypriane Ferrandina. Tonight's meeting with the fiery little Italian has been very satisfactory. The barber has talked freely; now Pinkerton wants to get the information down on paper in the privacy of his office. Taking his record book from the desk drawer, he writes:

> The conversation at once got into Politics, and Ferrandina who is a fine looking, intelligent appearing person, became very excited. . . . He has lived South for many years and is thoroughly imbued with the idea that the South must rule: that they (Southerners) have been outraged in their rights by the election of Lincoln, and freely justified resorting to any means ·

to prevent Lincoln from taking his seat, and as he spoke his eyes fairly glared and glistened, and his whole frame quivered, but he was fully conscious of all he was doing. He is a man well calculated for controlling and directing the ardent minded—he is an enthusiast, and believes that, to use his own words, "Murder of any kind is justifiable and right to save the rights of the Southern people."

11 CHEERING CROWDS
AND WILD COMMOTION
⋆ Saturday, February 16, 1861 ⋆

For this sixth day of the inaugural journey the train will travel through Ohio and a corner of Pennsylvania, arriving in Buffalo, New York, at 4:30 P.M. Escorted by the Cleveland Grays, a local military group, the Presidential party is driven to the Cleveland, Painesville, and Ashtabula Railroad station.

Exactly at nine o'clock the Special heads out northeast, running along the shores of Lake Erie. During the five-minute stop at Painesville, Ohio, Mr. Lincoln goes to the rear platform to greet the cheering crowd. "Ladies and gentlemen," he says, "I have stepped upon this platform that I may see you and that you may see me, and in the arrangement I have the best of the bargain."

The people clap hilariously.

Looking over toward a group of uniformed musicians, he adds, "Let us have the better music of the band." The musicians have time for only a few bars before the conductor cries, "All aboard!"

and the train pulls away from the station with Mr. Lincoln still bowing and waving.

Returning to his seat, the President-elect takes a few minutes to look over the newspapers that have earlier been delivered. He is particularly anxious to read the *Cleveland Plain Dealer,* for it was with Joseph W. Gray, the editor, that last night he had an interview. Although Mr. Gray is known to be an anti-Lincoln man, the conversation was pleasant enough. Turning quickly to the editorial page, Lincoln smiles. "We must confess," writes the editor, "to being most favorably impressed. If mistakes do occur in the Executive government of our country, we are satisfied they will not be charged to design."

A roistering crowd of some four thousand townspeople awaits the Special when it slows down for Ashtabula. Responding to the noisy greeting, Mr. Lincoln's words are barely audible. "I can only say how do you do, and farewell," he rasps, "as my voice, you perceive, will warrant nothing more. I am happy to see so many pleasant faces around me and to be able to greet you as friends."

Turning to reenter the coach, Mr. Lincoln hears a woman's voice asking to see the First Lady. Smiling, he replies, "I should hardly hope to induce her to appear, as I have always found it difficult to make her do what she did not want to."

At the last stop in Ohio—Conneaut—the many waiting spectators surge forward when the train comes to a halt. Although Mr. Lincoln's voice is now little more than a rough whisper, he knows these people have come a great distance to hear him speak. He stands silent for a moment and then wheezes, "I have lost my voice and cannot make a speech, but my intentions are good." He concludes by thanking everyone for the "kindly demonstration."

When the train commences moving slowly forward through the throng that lines both sides of the track, an old man calls out, "Don't give up the ship!" Mr. Lincoln responds quickly, "With your aid, I never will as long as life lasts."

After crossing the Ohio border, the Special winds through the wooded terrain of the Pennsylvania hills until it reaches Girard. Here an unexpected passenger comes aboard—Horace Greeley, owner and editor of the *New York Tribune*. Known for his admonition, "Go West, young man, go West!" Greeley is one of the most influential newspapermen in the United States and a dynamic force in the Republican party. He is on his way to Erie, Pennsylvania, he says, to deliver a lecture. Mr. Lincoln welcomes his political ally warmly, and for the next fifteen miles the two men engage in earnest conversation. As Mr. Greeley leaves the train at Erie, the President-elect suggests that he join the Special for Monday's trip to Albany.

The engines are changed at Erie, and the members of the party go to an upstairs dining room in the depot for their noontime meal. Enthusiastic crowds outside keep calling for Mr. Lincoln; once he has finished eating, he steps outside on the second-floor balcony. Still very hoarse, he excuses himself from making a speech but says that when the time comes for speaking, he will "say nothing not in accordance with the Constitution and the Laws and the manifest interest of the whole country." Despite the brevity of his remarks, he is loudly cheered.

Chugging away northeastward, the Special makes a short stop at Northeast, Pennsylvania, before crossing into the state of New York. When the train reaches Westfield, Mr. Lincoln sees a huge banner stretched above the tracks bearing the words:

WELCOME ABRAHAM LINCOLN TO THE
EMPIRE STATE

He appears on the rear platform, and after the wild huzzas have subsided, the President-elect says: "Some three months ago, I received a letter from a young lady here; it was a very pretty letter, and she advised me to let my whiskers grow, as it would improve my personal appearance; acting partly upon her suggestion, I have done so; and now, if she is here, I would like to see her."

A small boy, sitting on a nearby post, cries out, "There's Grace Bedell, Mr. Lincoln!" and points to a pretty little black-eyed girl who is blushing with embarrassment. The President-elect steps down off the platform, and the crowd parts courteously

as he makes his way toward her. Lifting Grace up in his long arms, he kisses her on the cheek; the audience shouts approval.

The next stop is Dunkirk, New York, a thriving port on Lake Erie. A triumphal arch has been erected over the track with the Union mottoes emblazoned on it. Military bands, armed companies of soldiers, and nearly fifteen thousand people have gathered here. When the train comes to a halt, the President-elect walks over to a velvet-covered platform erected beside a flag pole. He moves quickly to the national emblem and, touching the pole, says: "Standing as I do with my hand upon this staff, and under the folds of the American flag, I ask you to stand by me so long as I stand by it."

There are instant shouts of "We will! We will!" and wild applause as Mr. Lincoln reenters the coach.

Colonel Lamon suggests that it would be wise if the President-elect were permitted to rest for the next hour, in preparation for the events planned in Buffalo. Mr. Lincoln appreciates this short span of relaxation and buries himself in today's newspapers.

Promptly at three o'clock the train puffs into the Exchange Street station at Buffalo, where the rear car is halted opposite the main passenger entrance. Mr. Lincoln is greeted by former President Millard Fillmore, who heads the welcoming committee. The throngs inside the depot are excited at the sight of a former President with a President-elect; they shove forward to get a better look. Suddenly the crowd is out of control. Guards find themselves overwhelmed as the roaring mass pushes in from both sides upon the two distinguished men.

For several minutes there is wild confusion; the white-haired former President and the lanky President-elect sway back and forth while the crowd surges around them. In an attempt to protect Mr. Lincoln, Major David Hunter has his shoulder dislocated. There is very real danger that people will be crushed to death by the enthusiastic mob. With a desperate effort Colonel Lamon uses his bulky frame to get Mr. Lincoln and Mr. Fillmore to the waiting carriage.

The guards are now able to effect a semblance

of order, and the procession begins moving, preceded by a military band and a company of light artillerymen. Up Exchange Street and along Main the parade proceeds, passing thousands of flag-waving spectators.

The Presidential party is to stay at the American House. A few minutes before their arrival, a wagon filled with a half cord of wood draws up near the hotel entrance. The driver gets out, unloads the wood, and sets up his sawbuck. These actions are in fulfillment of an election bet made by two local citizens. If Mr. Lincoln were elected, the loser agreed to saw the wood in front of the hotel and present it to the poorest family in the city. If Mr. Lincoln had not been elected, the other party to the bet would have sawed the wood and given it to the *Buffalo Express,* a pro-Lincoln newspaper.

When the carriage stops at the American House, the sawing begins. Police and militia form a protective line from the street to the hotel entrance, and the President-elect is escorted inside without further trouble.

Almost immediately he appears on the second-floor balcony to be welcomed by the mayor. Still very hoarse, Mr. Lincoln responds in a rasping voice:

"Your worthy Mayor has been pleased to mention in his address to me, the fortunate and agreeable journey which I have had from home, on my rather circuitous route to the Federal Capital. . . . It is true we have had nothing, thus far, to mar the pleasure of the trip. . . ."

The irritating noise of the sawing continues, but Mr. Lincoln pays no attention to it.

"When we speak of threatened difficulties to the country, it is natural that there should be expected from me something with regard to particular measures. . . . when it is considered that these difficulties are without precedent, and have never been acted upon by any individual situated as I am, it is most proper I should wait, see the developments, and get all the light I can, so that when I do speak authoritatively I may be as near right as possible."

There is hearty applause, drowning out for the moment the persistent sawing noise. Mr. Lincoln concludes:

"You, as a portion of the great American people, need only to maintain your composure. Stand up to your sober convictions of right, to your obligations to the Constitution, act in accordance with those sober convictions, and the clouds which now arise in the horizon will be dispelled, and we shall have a bright and glorious future. . . ."

The acclamation is deafening as Mr. Lincoln reenters the hotel. When the evening meal is over, he holds a reception which has been billed as "open to the public." In spite of the cold snowy night, thousands of people come for the pleasure of shaking hands with the man who will soon be in the White House. To the children who file by with their parents, Mr. Lincoln pays special attention, patting them on the head and occasionally lifting a small one into his arms for a moment.

After the reception ends, a German choral society—the Saengerbund—appears to serenade the President-elect. When the song fest is over, Mr. Lincoln is escorted to his suite, bone-weary from an exhausting day. Glancing out the window, he is heartened by the sight of the banner extending across the front of the Young Men's Christian Union building on the opposite side of the street. The words on it are in reply to his Springfield farewell address:

WE WILL PRAY FOR YOU!

In his room at the American House Henry Villard is writing his dispatch for the *New York Herald*.

> The President has every reason to feel flattered and encouraged by the demonstrations in his honor. . . . He must have spoken at least fifty times during the week. In the kindness of his heart—not from any love of adulation, for he was really very awkward about it—he never refused to respond to a call for his appearance wherever the train stopped.

12 RUMORS, CONFIRMED
✶ Sunday, February 17, 1861 ✶

It's been a hectic week—all the speeches, receptions, parades, and travel. This seventh day of the inaugural journey promises to be a pleasant interlude. Members of the Presidential party are content to stay in their hotel rooms, relaxing and catching up on correspondence.

Captain George Hazzard, a member of the military detail, writes his wife: "As to your joining us, I fear it will be impractical, as Mr. and Mrs. Lincoln are worked almost out of their lives by visitors of both sexes. Every village sends a reception committee of twenty or thirty and some of them bring their wives, so that not only are all the seats in the cars taken, but the passway is filled with people standing."

In a letter to his fiancée, John Nicolay, Lincoln's private secretary, comments on yesterday's activities: "Arrived at the hotel, all was confusion. . . . We took matters into our own hands. . . . I don't know when I have done so much work as yesterday and I am feeling the effects of it today. The best criterion I can give you of my situation is the appearance of this letter. . . ."

The President-elect is leafing through the newspapers which have been brought to his suite. An editorial in the *New York Herald* catches his eye. James Gordon Bennett has written:

> Abraham Lincoln, as President-elect of the United States, is in a fair way to lose that high reputation which he gained in his Illinois stumping campaign of 1858 with Judge Douglas, as a candidate for the United States Senate. Since his departure from Springfield, en route for the White House, he has made several little speeches, but in none of them has he manifested the disposition or the capacity to grapple manfully with the dangers of this crisis in reference to the restoration of the Union, or the maintenance of the peace of the country. . . . If Mr. Lincoln has nothing better to offer upon this fearful crisis than the foolish consolations of his speech at Columbus, let him say nothing at all.

Despite such caustic editorials, the President-elect is determined to continue his present policy. He is prudent about what he says in these speeches during this journey because he does not want to be misrepresented. In his inaugural address he will speak out firmly. Only then can he speak with authority.

At ten o'clock the carriage of the former Chief Executive draws up at the American House. Millard Fillmore calls for Mr. Lincoln and takes him to a service at the Unitarian Church on Franklin

and Eagle streets. After listening to a sermon delivered by the Reverend George W. Hosmer, the
two men return to the hotel. There they are joined
by Mrs. Lincoln, and the three drive to Mr. Fillmore's residence on Niagara Square. Mrs. Lincoln
has long admired the former Chief Executive and
enjoys this opportunity to become better acquainted. The Sunday dinner in quiet surroundings
is a welcome change for the couple from Illinois.

Shortly after two o'clock the Lincolns return to
the hotel. Tad and Willie are having a lively game
of leapfrog in the family suite with the hotel
owner's son. The President-elect executes several
leaps himself to prove to the boys that he is still
agile. But the fun is soon interrupted by the arrival of visitors. Regretfully Mr. Lincoln leaves the
children and turns his attention to the callers.

During the Sunday evening supper, served in
the family suite, John Nicolay comes to tell the
family he has been in consultation with Mr. Wood,
the superintendent of arrangements. It seems that
the New York Central's division manager has suggested that tomorrow morning's departure hour be
set at five forty-five, instead of the scheduled
hour of six, in order to avoid "a repetition of
Saturday's crush." The Lincolns agree this is a
wise move and promise to be ready on time.

Before long, Millard Fillmore returns to the hotel
and accompanies Mr. Lincoln to a lecture in St.
James Hall. Father John Beeson is speaking there
in behalf of the American Indians. He has traveled

extensively through the West and has been horrified by the inhuman acts committed against the
Indians. The former President and the President-
elect listen attentively and compliment Father
Beeson afterward on his humanitarian work.

On this comparatively quiet Sunday evening,
Judge David Davis is writing to his wife, Sarah.
"The whole trip from Indianapolis to this City,"
he reports, "has been an Ovation such as has never
been witnessed in this Country. It is simply aston-
ishing. The people seem wild with excitement everywhere, & turn out in large masses everywhere."

As the judge puts the letter into an envelope, he
cannot help wondering what events will take place
during the next six days. It has been a grueling
journey thus far, and there are many more and
still larger cities to visit. Already he is exhausted.
Mr. Lincoln must have a remarkable constitution
to endure all this and much more to come.

Meanwhile, in Baltimore, Allan Pinkerton has
also spent an exhausting day. Early this morning
Operative Harry Davies came to the Front Street
office with a detailed report of a secret meeting
he had attended last night. O. K. Hillard, the pro-
Southern fanatic with whom he had become good
friends, issued the invitation. When Davies arrived at the designated spot, he found about
twenty men there. Some he had met before; others
he had never seen.

He was introduced to the leader, Cypriano Ferrandina, the barber from Barnum's Hotel with

whom Pinkerton had talked on Friday night. Ferrandina welcomed the newcomer by saying that their mutual friend, Hillard, had said many fine things about Davies.

After all the doors were locked, the leader announced the purpose of the meeting. Plans, he said, must now be completed to see that Abraham Lincoln would not leave Baltimore alive. He then began to describe in detail Mr. Lincoln's itinerary —precisely what time the President-elect would arrive next Saturday and what arrangements had been made to transport him across the city.

The narrow pedestrian tunnel at the Calvert Street Station, through which the President-elect would necessarily walk to reach his carriage, was to be the deathtrap. Ferrandina further confided that when Mr. Lincoln's train arrived, a disturbance would occur in another part of the station. The police, if any were present, would run to quell the outbreak, leaving the tunnel completely unprotected. There would undoubtedly be many people in the walkway, eager for a look at the President-elect; this would therefore be the perfect time for the assassin to carry out his mission, using either a dagger or a gun. The choice of a weapon would be left to the killer.

The leader had then announced that all those present were to be in the tunnel next Saturday, that among them would be the lucky person designated to kill Mr. Lincoln. Who that privileged man would be was now to be decided by drawing ballots out of a hat.

All the ballots, Ferrandina said, were white—with one exception. Whoever drew the red ballot was to commit the murder. Escape afterward would be a simple matter. A small steamer had already been chartered. The assassin would vanish in the crowd and make his way to Chesapeake Bay and the waiting ship. From there he would be taken to the safety of the Virginia shore.

Just before the drawing took place, Ferrandina cautioned the group not to reveal the color of the ballot each man drew, even if it proved to be white. Picking up a hat filled with pieces of paper, the leader then instructed the men to form a single line and step up, one at a time, to get a ballot. The gas lights were turned off; the drawing was held in complete darkness. The meeting broke up soon afterward; each man was anxious to be alone and find out the color of the paper he was holding.

Davies had left with his friend, Hillard, who boasted that there was no doubt whatsoever that the plot would succeed. The operative suggested that the man who had drawn the red ballot might lose his nerve at the last moment. But Hillard said, "No, that could never happen."

In a burst of confidence he had then sworn Davies to secrecy. There had not been just *one* red ballot, he whispered. To insure that Mr. Lincoln would never leave the tunnel alive, Ferrandina had put *eight* red ballots into the hat. Not one, but eight members of the group would thus be armed and ready to commit the murder.

Shocked though he was, Davies had pretended

to be pleased with the plot. Shortly after leaving Hillard, the operative had hurried to Allan Pinkerton with all the details.

Now that he knows how the plot is to be executed, the chief detective is somewhat relieved. At least, this is something definite; he can immediately begin working out a way to counter the plot and insure the President-elect's safety. There are only six days left before Mr. Lincoln is to reach Baltimore. Should he go directly to New York and speak to him personally?

After considering the matter from every angle, Pinkerton decides that it is wiser to stay here in Baltimore as long as possible. If any new developments arise, he'll be on hand to weigh their effects on his own plans. He will dispatch Mrs. Warne to New York City with a letter for Norman Judd. After all, Judd has been alerted to the possibilities; at this juncture it seems sensible not to alarm Mr. Lincoln.

Pinkerton takes some paper from his desk drawer and begins to write. At last he has some specific details, he informs Judd; the President-elect will be in grave danger if the plans to come through Baltimore on Saturday are not changed. Sometime—he doesn't yet know when—he will send word about a meeting place with Judd. They can map out a strategy together to counteract the plot. Meanwhile, he adds, the whole matter is strictly confidential. Please reveal nothing to the President-elect or anyone else.

After signing his name, the detective locks up his desk. He has accomplished as much as he can today. Early tomorrow morning he will see Mrs. Warne and ask her to take the 5:16 P.M. train to New York City. She will be his personal messenger in delivering the letter to Judd. There may be some difficulty in locating him, but Pinkerton has great confidence in Mrs. Warne's ability.

13 NEAR RIOT IN ALBANY
⋆ Monday, February 18, 1861 ⋆

The gaslights in the rooms at Buffalo's American House begin flickering long before daylight. The members of the Presidential party have risen very early to meet the new departure time of quarter to six. A company from the Seventy-fourth Regiment arrives at half past four, and a few moments later the Union Coronet Band appears to escort the party with patriotic tunes.

After the baggage has been loaded and the carriages filled, the procession moves through the empty streets, and Buffalo citizens are abruptly awakened by the lively music. Despite the snowy weather and the unseemly hour, several hundred persons have gathered at the depot for a cheerful send-off. Little time is lost in getting the passengers aboard, and the train moves away quickly amid shouts of farewell. Only one member of the family is missing from the rear coach. Robert has again been invited to ride in the locomotive cab and act as "assistant engineer," an honor that pleases the young man immensely.

The New York Central has taken special precautions for today's trip. During the past twenty-four hours employees have inspected every inch of the track over which the train will run on the 296 mile trip to Albany. Locomotives are fired up all along the route, ready to be used in case of an emergency. And the superintendent of the railroad's telegraph department is aboard, keeping in constant communication with other trains to insure a safe journey.

In the light of a gray dawn, the train pulls into Batavia. Though the hour is still early, a large group greets the Special with cannon salutes and calls for a speech. Mr. Lincoln answers by saying he does not desire "to appear before you or the country as a talker, nor to obtain a reputation as such." He thanks them for assembling at such an inconvenient hour. And their cheers ring out as he waves farewell.

The Special moves quickly into the snow-covered countryside. Small clusters of people are gathered beside the track, waving flags and lanterns, as the train passes; Mr. Lincoln is highly gratified by this show of interest. At Rochester he meets the town mayor and tells a record number massed around the tracks: "I confess myself, after having seen large audiences since leaving home, overwhelmed with this vast number of faces at this hour of the morning. . . ."

Impatient to be off, the engineer starts the train just as a small boy clambers up on the edge of the rear platform. "How do you do, Mr. Lincoln!" he says. The President-elect shakes his hand and shows parentlike concern for the little fellow by admonishing him to be careful in jumping off the moving train.

Syracuse is the next scheduled stop. Here a handsome structure has been erected in front of the Globe Hotel for the ceremonial greeting and response. Mr. Lincoln declines the honor, saying this is too much of a platform for his few words, and adds:

> ". . . though I am unwilling to go upon this platform, you are not at liberty to draw any inferences concerning any other platform with which my name has been or is connected . . ."

As the shouts of laughter diminish, he concludes:

> "I wish you a long life and prosperity individually, and pray that with the perpetuity of those institutions under which we have all so long lived and prospered, our happiness may be secured, our future made brilliant, and the glorious destiny of our country established forever."

A picnic lunch for the Presidential party is brought aboard, and the passengers are treated to what one of them describes as "a bountiful meal." Heavy snow is now falling, at times almost obscuring the farms and villages along the tracks. In spite of near blizzard conditions, a large crowd is waiting when the train makes its scheduled stop at Utica.

The students of Hamilton College have arrived from nearby Clinton to join in cheering the President-elect as he mounts a specially constructed flat car. Turning to the crowd, he says:

"I appear before you . . . to see you, and to allow you all to see me. At the same time I acknowledge, ladies, that I think I have the best of the bargain in the sight. . . ."

Like any politician, the President-elect likes to pay compliments. Though he has used this one before, he knows it pleases any group. And his confidence is not misplaced. He draws cheers and laughter with his words.

Only a few minutes after leaving Utica, Mrs. Lincoln motions to William Johnson, the Negro valet, and whispers to him. Johnson disappears toward the baggage car and a short time later returns carrying a handsome broadcloth overcoat and hatbox. Mrs. Lincoln persuades her husband to discard the worn-looking overcoat he has been wearing, as well as the weather-beaten stovepipe hat.

The New York Times reporter includes this incident in his daily dispatch, with the comment that Mr. Lincoln looks "fifty percent better." Then he adds, "If Mrs. Lincoln's advice is always as near right as it was in this instance, the country may congratulate itself upon the fact that its President-elect is a man who does not reject, even in important matters, the advice and counsel of his wife." Henry Villard of the *New York Herald* takes the opportunity to compliment William Johnson, writing that "the untiring vigilance with which he took care of the Presidential party is entitled to high credit."

When the train rolls into Little Falls, a village nestled in the Mohawk Valley, church bells peal out a welcome to the visitors. After Mr. Lincoln's brief remarks, a chorus of ladies wave their handkerchiefs as the band plays "Hail, Columbia."

Further stops are made at St. Johnsville, Palatine Bridge, Fonda, and Amsterdam. In Schenectady record crowds have gathered, and one of the cannon misfires. The train is accidentally hit, breaking windows and knocking out one of the doors in the first coach. Fortunately, no one is injured, but the mishap causes great consternation among Superintendent Woods, Colonel Lamon, and Colonel Ellsworth. Mr. Lincoln, however, pays no attention; he continues to address the crowd. So constant is the applause, one local reporter writes: "We were able to obtain only a few disjointed sentences of what the President-elect said."

A thunder of cannon fire from the heights above Albany heralds the approach of the Presidential Special. Promptly at twenty minutes past two the train rolls into the station. The enthusiastic crowd rushes forward. In their eagerness to catch a glimpse of Mr. Lincoln, some attempt to break into the rear coach where he is quietly waiting. Superintendent Woods goes to the rear platform

and surveys the wildly cheering mob—a mob that
the small cordon of local police is unable to control.

Company B of the Twenty-fifth Infantry Regiment has been appointed to escort the Presidential party into the city, but its members have not
yet appeared. Mayor Thatcher arrives, panting
with exhaustion after having been buffeted by the
crowds. He seeks out Superintendent Wood and
suggests they start the procession, but Wood refuses to let Mr. Lincoln leave the train until rein-
forcements can be brought.

For half an hour the mob surges back and forth.
Fighting breaks out among the spectators, and the
scattering of police have little effect in this wild
confrontation. When Company B finally shows up,

the soldiers begin wielding the clubs of their muskets in order to clear a small area around the train.

Once order has been partially restored, the President-elect emerges from the rear coach to be officially welcomed by Mayor Thatcher. The passengers climb into the waiting carriages, with Mr. Lincoln and the mayor leading the way. The streets, the steps, and the windows of all buildings for more than a mile are densely crowded. The President-elect stands erect in the carriage, bowing to the thousands who cheer him. The parade winds up the long hill toward the capitol grounds, passing a local theater where the actor John Wilkes Booth is starring in *The Apostate.*

From the steps of the capitol Mr. Lincoln thanks

the crowd for "this most hearty and magnificent welcome." He goes on to say that in any country where there is freedom of thought, citizens belong to different political parties. Then he observes:

> "And when an election is past, it is altogether befitting a free people, that until the next election, they should be as one people."

After he finishes, the President-elect is escorted to a joint session of the New York legislature. In response to the greeting of Governor Edwin D. Morgan, Mr. Lincoln emphasizes the point he has been making in all his scheduled addresses—that he will not speak of national policy until he has been sworn in as President of the United States.

> "When the time comes, I shall speak, as well as I am able, for the good of the present and future of this country. . . . In the meantime, if we have patience; if we restrain ourselves; if we allow ourselves not to run off in a passion, I still have confidence that the Almighty, the Maker of the Universe, will, through the instrumentality of this great and intelligent people, bring us through this as He has through all the other difficulties of our country."

Amid shouts and cheers, Mr. Lincoln leaves the legislature and goes to the executive mansion for dinner with Governor Morgan and his family. Afterward, the President-elect returns to Delavan House where two receptions are held in his honor: one for the general public in the hotel lobby, and another for the ladies whom Mrs. Lincoln is entertaining on the second floor.

It is very probable, however, that Mr. Lincoln's thoughts tonight are elsewhere. A short while ago he was told that news has come over the wireless of the ceremony that took place this afternoon in Montgomery, Alabama. In the portico of the state-house, Jefferson Davis has been inaugurated as president of the newly formed Confederate States of America.

The cryptic message stated only the fact. But the President-elect knows that Davis's inauguration means that the nation is now formally divided. The people of the United States are no longer controlled by a single national government. Mr. Lincoln is anxious to know exactly what Jefferson Davis has said. But he will have to wait for tomorrow's newspapers. The Southerners have chosen a political maneuver—peaceful secession. If this does not succeed, what is to stop them from resorting to force? Is civil war inevitable?

14 NEW YORK . . . AND
OMINOUS NEWS
★ Tuesday, February 19, 1861 ★

An unpredictable thaw has changed the schedule slightly for today's run to New York City. During the night great masses of ice have come hurtling down the Hudson River, demolishing bridges and putting the ferry out of commission.

At a quarter to eight the Presidential party leaves Delavan House and walks around the corner to the depot, accompanied by the mayor and a number of other city officials. They reboard the train which yesterday brought them into the city, and the Special heads northward on the Albany and Vermont tracks. Though time-consuming, the detour is necessary because of the ice jam.

Arriving at Green Island, the train turns eastward, crossing over the only railroad bridge spanning the Hudson River, and proceeds to Troy, New York. Word has spread quickly that the Special is to stop here—unexpectedly; almost ten thousand people have gathered to greet the visitors. Mr. Lincoln is pleased by the enthusiasm of the crowd and tells them he accepts "this flattering reception with feelings of profound gratefulness."

The passengers transfer to an all-new train provided by the Hudson River Railroad. Its rear coach has been built expressly for Mr. Lincoln, with lounges and arm chairs designed for his comfort. The car is equipped with heaters and ventilators; four wax-candle chandeliers with cut-glass globes provide illumination.

The railroad has taken extra precautions for today's trip to New York City. All personnel are on duty along the line, acting as flagmen and track guards. A pilot engine will once more precede the Special the entire distance. Samuel Sloan, president of the railroad, is aboard, as well as William Creamer, who invented the safety braking mechanism with which the cars are equipped.

Once settled in the rear coach, Mr. Lincoln reaches anxiously for the newspapers stacked beside his chair. Most editors have chosen to headline yesterday's events in parallel columns. In one is the story of the Albany visit and the plea of the President-elect: "If we have patience, if we restrain ourselves, if we allow ourselves not to run off in a passion, I still have confidence. . . ." Alongside is the account of the extraordinary event that took place yesterday in Montgomery, Alabama. Jefferson Davis is quoted as sounding a warning note: "If the passion or lust of dominion should cloud the judgement or inflame the ambition of these States, we must prepare to meet the emergency and maintain by . . . the sword, the position which we have assumed among the nations of the earth."

There are further disturbing reports. In the most prominent theater in Montgomery, an actress named Maggie Mitchell executed a flag dance, "trampling the Stars and Stripes beneath her nimble feet," and the audience was said to have been "yelling with pleasure." In other Confederate cities the American flag was buried with funeral dirges and the singing of a new song, "Farewell to the Star-Spangled Banner."

Mr. Lincoln stares silently out the window. As the train winds down beside the frozen Hudson River, he is heartened by the sight of skaters who pause to wave flags and cheer as the Special passes.

At Poughkeepsie Mr. Lincoln tells the eager spectators:

> "It is with your aid, as the people, that I think we shall be able to preserve—not the country, for the country will preserve itself, but the institutions of the country—those institutions which have made us free, intelligent and happy—the most free, the most intelligent and the happiest people on the globe. . . ."

There is tremendous applause, everyone shouting and clapping at one time.

Mrs. Lincoln, sitting in the coach beside one of the windows, is suddenly spotted by the crowd. She is given a warm welcome and opens the window to return the salutation.

"Where are the children? Show us the children," someone shouts.

Mrs. Lincoln turns and motions for Robert and Willie to come to the window. There is more cheering, and someone else calls, "Have you any more on board?"

"Yes, there's another," replies Mrs. Lincoln as she turns away to summon Tad. But the youngest member of the family throws himself on the floor, heels kicking high in the air, and refuses to budge. Laughingly his mother returns to the window and explains that the "pet of the family" does not want to be put on exhibition.

Aboard the Special today is one of New York State's leading politicians, Thurlow Weed. After the train leaves Poughkeepsie, Mr. Weed asks the President-elect where he plans to stay in Washington before the inaugural. A house has already been rented, Mr. Lincoln explains.

Weed frowns thoughtfully for a moment. In all honesty, he says, he thinks that it would be wiser for the President-elect and his family to be in a hotel. Willard's would be a good possibility—very centrally located on Pennsylvania Avenue. Mr. Lincoln agrees and asks Weed to make the arrangements, adding: "The truth is, I suppose I am now public property; and a public inn is the place where people can have access to me."

There are two more speaking stops—one at Fishkill and another at Peekskill—before the scream of the whistle announces the arrival of the Special

at three o'clock in New York City. The train halts
at the Hudson River Railroad's new depot on Thir-
tieth Street. President Sloan explains it was hurried to completion so that Mr. Lincoln might be
its first visitor.

The party is conducted through the station and
out to the waiting carriages. The President-elect,
after being greeted by Superintendent of Police
John Kennedy, climbs into an open barouche
drawn by a team of six black horses. The crowd
outside the depot is larger than any he has yet
encountered. But the enthusiasm of the people is
distinctly less than in Buffalo or Albany. There are
cheers, but not from everyone. At times the people
only gawk at their distinguished visitor; some
even appear sullen and hostile. There is no military escort, no band, not even a bugle corps.

New Yorkers are somewhat fearful of this un-
known backwoodsman from Illinois who is soon
to become President of the United States. Will he
compromise on the extension of Negro slavery?
Or will there be a war? Through the efforts of
hard-driving business men, the city has become
the commercial center of the nation. The South
owes more than $170,000,000 to local firms and
banks. Armed conflict could mean financial ruin
for the metropolis. Public officials here have re-
peatedly stated that New York City should estab-
lish itself as a free city, separate from the Union,
and continue its trade, uninterrupted, with every
section of the country.

Knowing the anti-Lincoln sentiments of many citizens, Police Superintendent Kennedy has done everything possible to insure Mr. Lincoln's safety. Thirteen hundred uniformed members of the metropolitan police line the three-and-a-half-mile route to the Astor House at 222 Broadway, between Barclay and Vesey streets, where the Presidential party will stay. When the procession turns into Twenty-third Street, the applause and the demonstrations become more enthusiastic. Near Eighth Avenue a banner stretched across the street proclaims:

FEAR NOT, ABRAHAM, I AM THY SHIELD
AND THY EXCEEDING GREAT STRENGTH

Flags are flying; business houses, residences, and newspaper offices are decked with red, white, and blue bunting. Church bells peal out in welcome as the parade passes.

Along Broadway there is a dense mass of people, anxious for a look at the President-elect. All traffic has been halted; omnibus drivers have parked their vehicles on nearby streets and sold standing space on the roofs to eager onlookers.

Two hundred policemen from the Sixteenth Precinct are holding the street open in front of the Astor House. Spectators are permitted only on the sidewalk opposite. Diagonally across from the hotel is P. T. Barnum's Museum of Oddities; the enterprising manager has sold tickets for standing room in the windows and on the balconies of

his building. A band on the roof entertains the crowd while they wait for the procession to arrive. When Mr. Lincoln's carriage reaches the front of the Astor House, the throng surges forward. Everyone wants a closer look, but the police lines hold firm.

The poet Walt Whitman is one of those who observe the proceedings from the top of an omnibus. Whipping out his notebook, he jots down his impressions:

> A tall figure stepp'd out of the center of these barouches, paus'd leisurely on the sidewalk, look'd up at the granite walls and looming architecture of the grand old hotel—then, after a relieving stretch of arms and legs, turn'd round for over a minute to slowly and good-humoredly scan the appearance of the vast and silent crowds.

Another person, watching from an upstairs window in the Astor House, is Mrs. Kate Warne. She arrived early this morning with the letter from Detective Pinkerton. Now that the Presidential party is here, she hastens to write a note to Mr. Judd, asking him to come to her room as soon as possible. She calls a bellboy and instructs him to deliver the note immediately.

Through the line of police guarding the entrance, stairway, and halls, the President-elect is conducted to the suite of four rooms reserved for him and his family. There he turns to shake hands with Police Superintendent Kennedy and to compliment him on the splendid way in which his men have performed. The superintendent replies that he has only been doing his duty. "Well," says Mr. Lincoln, "a man ought to be thanked when he does his duty right well."

Meanwhile, the bellboy has returned to Kate Warne's room to inform her that Mr. Judd is not with the Presidential party. He missed the train at Albany but is expected to arrive before long. As soon as he registers, he will be given her note.

Outside the hotel the crowd is wedged tightly across the width of the street. There are continual shouts for the President-elect. Mr. Lincoln is holding an informal reception, but he excuses himself momentarily to appear on the small balcony above the entrance. He is still hoarse, so he tells the crowd that he has no speech to make and begs to be excused for the present.

Returning to the parlor, the President-elect continues greeting visitors until almost six o'clock. After an elegant meal served to a select group of guests, there are still more local celebrities to meet. William Cullen Bryant, the poet and editor of the *New York Evening Post,* introduces Mayor Fernando Wood who wants to extend his personal welcome to Mr. Lincoln before the official ceremonies take place tomorrow at City Hall.

It is shortly after half past seven when Norman Judd knocks on Mrs. Warne's door. She asks him to come in and hands him the letter from Pinkerton. After reading it, he is obviously upset and begins asking question after question. Mrs. Warne refuses to answer, saying that she cannot discuss the matter.

Judd is thoroughly alarmed. He would like to show this letter to several members of the Presidential party and consult with the New York police. Mrs. Warne advises him against any such action, cautioning that he must say nothing but keep his composure and talk with Pinkerton first.

Couldn't Pinkerton come to New York if they wired him tonight? Judd wants to know. The operative explains that the detective wants to remain in Baltimore until the last possible moment to find out all he can. Besides, this is Tuesday night. It would be impossible for him to reach New York for any kind of a conference before the Presidential party leaves for Philadelphia on Thursday morning.

Judd recalls that Vice-President-elect Hannibal Hamlin will be arriving from his home in Maine tomorrow afternoon. Surely he should be consulted about this letter. Again Mrs. Warne shakes her head. No, the contents must be kept strictly confidential. She explains that she herself is leaving for Baltimore tomorrow morning and will gladly deliver any message Judd may want to send to her chief.

A sharp knock interrupts the conversation. When Mrs. Warne opens the door, she is handed a telegram. Tearing open the envelope, she reads aloud:

Tell Judd I mean all I said and that today they are
offering ten for one and twenty for two.
                                    (Signed) Hutchinson

Judd is aghast. The detective's wire obviously
means that he is referring to the betting odds on
Mr. Lincoln's reaching Washington alive. As a
friend, Norman Judd is deeply concerned about the
safety of the President-elect. He knows, however,
that there is an even greater cause for alarm; now
that the secessionists have formed the Confederacy, the country is being torn apart. If Mr. Lincoln were to be assassinated, the nation might be
plunged into civil war overnight. Perhaps such a
war is already inevitable. But should it happen,
there must be a strong man in the White House.
Until Mr. Lincoln is inaugurated, he has no authority; he cannot exercise the leadership the country
must have in such a crisis.

Judd again pleads with Mrs. Warne to allow him
to consult with Vice-President-elect Hamlin, but
her answer remains a firm no. Then will she do
what she can to persuade Pinkerton to meet him
in Philadelphia? Judd asks. This she *can* promise—and does. The two shake hands and bid each
other a hasty farewell.

In a large room on the first floor of the Astor
House, extensive preparations have been made for
Mr. Lincoln to greet more than four hundred local
campaign workers. At eight thirty tonight he is
escorted into the huge gathering by E. Delafield

Smith, chairman of the Republican Central Committee. To introduce his famous guest, Mr. Smith says: "It is a remarkable incident that there should have been but two receptions in this room. One was to Daniel Webster, the other to Henry Clay, and a third is now to Abraham Lincoln." The guests cheer lustily.

Obviously pleased, the President-elect responds with an impromptu speech:

> "I have not kept silent since the Presidential election from any party craftiness, or from any indifference to the anxieties that pervade the minds of men about the aspect of the political affairs of this country. I have kept silence for the reason that I supposed it was peculiarly proper that I should do so until the time came when, according to the customs of the country, I should speak officially. . . . And now, my friends, I have said enough."

There are cries of "No, no," and "Go on, go on," but Mr. Lincoln only smiles and waves. Several nearby policemen form a cordon around him, and they start moving to the stairway. Overhearing some campaign workers remark they would like to shake his hand, the President-elect says that he will be happy to oblige. A line forms quickly; each person who files by receives a hearty handclasp and an expression of gratitude for his service during the campaign.

It is nearly ten o'clock when the reception ends. Mr. Lincoln bids his friends good night and is taken to his suite by a special detail of police. On the streets around the hotel, metropolitan officers stand guard throughout the night.

In the editor's office of the *New York Herald*, James Gordon Bennett is describing today's events. "The masses of the people did not turn out," he writes. "There was a faint cheer as Mr. Lincoln entered his carriage at the railway station, but none of those spontaneous movements for which our people are noted."

The *New York World* reporter, however, in reviewing these identical events, chooses to ignore the hostility and to emphasize the enthusiasm of the majority. "There was not the slightest insult either by word or action offered to the distinguished guest. This is remarkable when the state of political feeling existing all over the country is considered . . . and is in marked contrast with the disturbances in European capitals in times of great political excitement."

15 ODDITIES, RECEPTIONS, AND OPERA
★ Wednesday, February 20, 1861 ★

Phineas T. Barnum, merchant of oddities, has placed several advertisements in this morning's New York newspapers. They read:

PRESIDENT ABRAHAM LINCOLN has informed Mr. Barnum that he will positively VISIT THIS MUSEUM THIS DAY. Those who would see him should come early.

Although Barnum kept popping in and out of yesterday's reception at the Astor House, telling Mr. Lincoln he must be sure to visit the museum, the President-elect has declined all invitations. He will not, he says, be put on exhibition "for a twenty-five cent admission charge." Nevertheless, hundreds of people are lining up outside Barnum's Museum early this morning, hoping to catch a glimpse of the newly elected President of the United States.

The only Lincoln they see, however, is Robert, who cannot resist strolling through the museum.

He is enticed by "the wonderful sea horse, the popular man-monkey and the celebrated Aztec children," which are featured this week.

While Mr. Lincoln breakfasts with several of New York's leading merchants at the home of Moses H. Grinnell, politicians and reporters gather in the corridors of the Astor House. Little Tad suddenly appears and marches about "full of spirits," blowing on a paper trumpet. When someone asks what his name is, the youngster shouts "Lincoln" through the homemade instrument and capers off to his own music.

Returning to his suite, the President-elect finds his reception room filled with visitors. Among them is the Honorable Joshua Dewey, a ninety-four-year-old gentleman, to whom Mr. Lincoln gives his undivided attention. Dewey says that he enlisted in the Revolutionary Army when he was fifteen, cast his first ballot for George Washington, and has voted in every election since that time. He's the oldest living graduate of Yale University and has served in the New York legislature. When he adds that he voted for "Honest Abe" last November, he receives a hearty handshake from Mr. Lincoln.

At eleven o'clock Alderman Charles G. Cornell and a committee from the Common Council call for the President-elect to take him to City Hall where Mayor Wood extends the formal greetings of the metropolis. In response, Mr. Lincoln says:

"There is nothing that can ever bring me willingly to

consent to the destruction of this Union, under which not only the commercial city of New York, but the whole country has acquired its greatness . . . So long, then, as it is possible that the prosperity and the liberties of the people can be preserved in the Union, it shall be my purpose at all times to preserve it."

Mayor Wood then introduces his guest of honor to the members of the council and other city officials. Afterward, the doors are opened, and the public reception begins. Hundreds, eager to meet the President-elect, pour through the double lines of police. When a tall hawk-faced man says, "I've been told I look like you," Mr. Lincoln shakes his hand with vigor. "Then it's all settled," he quips, "you're a handsome man!"

A portly woman carrying a faded umbrella approaches, pulling a bored-looking male behind her. "This is my husband," she says proudly, "and you must shake hands with him, for he is a member of the Indiana legislature."

"He might have come from a worse state," is Mr. Lincoln's answer, "but he could not have a better half."

A few moments later a middle-aged gentleman files by. "If you satisfy the people this time, Mr. Lincoln," he says, "you will receive the unanimous vote of the next electoral college."

The smile disappears from the face of the President-elect. "I think when the clouds look as dark as they do now," he replies grimly, "one term might satisfy any man."

At times two people reach the guest of honor simultaneously, and Mr. Lincoln extends both hands. The room grows hot, and Mayor Wood suggests that perhaps they should stop the endless line. Mr. Lincoln says no, that he will shake hands until noon; after that for another hour the people can merely pass by. Police instruct the waiting crowd outside, but even after twelve o'clock, the President-elect makes some exceptions. When a white-haired gentleman steps up and says, "I came forty-mile to do it, but never mind," Mr. Lincoln is unable to resist. He reaches down and gives the old man a cordial handshake.

At one o'clock the doors are closed, and the guest of honor is taken back to the Astor House. He had hoped for an hour's rest; instead, his reception room is again filled with visitors. One of the callers is Knox the hatter, who presents Mr. Lincoln with a handsome silk top hat. Word of the gift circulates throughout the hotel, and very soon the Astor House hatter, Leary, sends up for the President-elect's measurements. It is only a matter of minutes before the messenger returns with Mr. Leary's finest wool hat. Watching Mr. Lincoln's pleasure as he tries on first one hat and then the other, a reporter standing nearby asks which he prefers. To a skilled politician, the question poses no difficulty. "They mutually surpass each other," Mr. Lincoln answers.

Young Willie, accompanied by Officer Dolan of the Second Precinct, spends the afternoon at Barnum's Museum of Oddities. Tad has refused to go. His excuse is that he can see plenty of bears in the country he came from, and he doesn't want to waste time at "that old museum." People who had hoped to scc the President-elect at the exhibits seize the opportunity to shake Willie's hand instead.

Shortly before six o'clock Vice-President-elect Hamlin and his wife arrive and check in at the Astor House. Because the Lincoln and Hamlin families are not well acquainted, a quiet dinner has been planned. Once it begins, the atmosphere is somewhat stilted until a plate of oysters on the half shell is placed before each guest. Looking at the oysters with a quizzical expression, Mr. Lin-

coln says, "Well, I don't know that I can manage these things, but I guess I can learn." The home-spun remark evokes general laughter, putting everyone at ease, and the dinner party is a pleasant one.

While the elder Lincolns entertain their guests, Willie and Tad are getting ready to go to Laura Keene's Theater. The feature attractions tonight are the play *Seven Sisters* and a patriotic tableau *Uncle Sam's Magic Lantern.* For the past three hours Tad has pestered the nurse who will escort them. "It will be all over before we get there," he keeps saying, "so please make haste."

After dinner, Mrs. Lincoln and Mrs. Hamlin

walk toward the ladies' parlor and hold a reception for some five hundred guests. Later this evening a *New York Herald* reporter describes the First Lady. "Mrs. Lincoln's smile," he writes, "is a very pleasant and amiable one, and all who had the pleasure of seeing her . . . and witnessing her frank, easy, and lady-like manner, agree that she would fill with ease and dignity the high position to which she will shortly be called."

The President-elect has promised to attend a performance at the New York Academy of Music. Shortly after eight o'clock, Judge Davis and Alderman Cornell call for him, and they depart for the handsome new building on Fourteenth Street and Irving Place.

The opera tonight is Giuseppe Verdi's latest—*Un ballo in maschera*—its libretto dealing with the murder of a ruler. Signor Muzio, impresario and conductor, has publicly announced that Mr. Lincoln will be there, and long before the curtain rises, some three thousand members of New York society are in their seats, peering eagerly around for the distinguished visitor.

The first act has already begun when the Lincoln party arrives; they slip into a private box on the second tier. Although the performance continues without interruption, many people twist and turn searching for Mr. Lincoln. Once he is discovered, the news is whispered from one to another. When the curtain comes down at the end of the first act, there is loud applause, and the cast takes several curtain calls. But the hand-clapping and cheering only become louder; obviously the audience has found Mr. Lincoln. At first he bows from his seat, but when shout after shout continues, the tall figure stands and waves to the audience.

At that moment the curtain rises. The entire cast of the opera is assembled on the stage in front of a magnificent flag. They begin singing "The Star-Spangled Banner," and the people in the audience jump to their feet to join in the patriotic song. Mr. Lincoln gestures toward the colors and sings with the audience. He is deeply moved by this spontaneous tribute.

After the second act, Judge Davis suggests that the Presidential party depart quietly. Mr. Lincoln is visibly tired. If they leave now, perhaps he can get some rest. Tomorrow will be another long day.

It is precisely eight o'clock on this eleventh day of the inaugural journey when Mr. Lincoln and his party emerge from the private entrance of the Astor House. The departure has been publicly announced for nine o'clock, but last night the plans were changed; it was decided to leave an hour earlier, in order to avoid the crowds that swarm around the President-elect wherever he appears. Within a few minutes the carriages are filled and clatter off toward the Cortlandt Street dock.

Waiting at the pier is the gaily decorated ferryboat, *John P. Jackson,* with a welcoming committee from New Jersey. When the procession arrives, the gangplank is lowered, and the carriages are driven aboard while a band plays patriotic tunes. As Mr. Lincoln steps down, he is greeted by A. A. Hardenberg, president of Jersey City's Board of Aldermen. The moorings are cast off, and the ferryboat gets underway.

After an informal reception in the cabin below, the President-elect expresses a desire to go up on the bridge. Rather than take a direct course, the pilot heads out toward Bedloe's Island and then turns west to the Jersey City terminal. The harbor is alive with steamers, brigs, tugs, schooners, and barges. Whistles shriek, guns boom, seamen wave flags as the *John P. Jackson* steams by. Mr. Lincoln is excited by the panorama of ships and says he hopes he may sometime have "a fuller and more extended view" of the harbor.

After the ferry has been docked and the gangplank lowered, the party is conducted into the depot of the New Jersey Railroad. It is a tremendous structure with a very high ceiling. Around the interior runs a huge gallery, which today is reserved for ladies only. Men throng the floor below. Some twenty-five thousand people have gathered here to welcome the Presidential party.

A flatcar in the center of the building has been converted into a stage, "carpeted and hung with red, white, and blue trimming." When Mr. Lincoln enters, the applause is ear-splitting as it reverberates through the depot. Few hear the welcoming speech, but the crowd quiets down when the President-elect responds by thanking the people for "this very kind and cordial reception—not as given to me individually, but as to the representative of the Chief Magistracy of this great nation."

When he finishes, there is a rush forward to shake Mr. Lincoln's hand. The police guard surrounding the flatcar is overwhelmed. The officers attempt to push back the mob, but to no avail. Mr. Lincoln is hemmed in. Colonel Ellsworth suggests that perhaps a second speech—this one, a salute to the ladies—may calm the crowd. The President-elect once more comes to the front of the platform and again uses the compliment that he has repeated many times—one that is certain to please. He says that from his position, especially after looking around the gallery, he feels that he has "decidedly the best of the bargain." Laughingly the people give way, and the party moves out to the waiting train.

Meanwhile, in Philadelphia there is an air of suppressed excitement. This afternoon the President-elect and his party are to arrive. The city is well prepared. Homes and business houses are gay with tricolor bunting; American flags float gently in the light breeze. Most of the police force has been assigned to guard the parade route.

Early this morning Allan Pinkerton came to Philadelphia and checked in at the St. Louis House under the alias of J. H. Hutchinson. He suggests to Mrs. Kate Warne, who has accompanied him, that she wait in her room for further instructions while he straightens out certain matters before meeting with Norman Judd. First of all, he wants to reach Mr. Felton, president of the Philadelphia, Wilmington and Baltimore Railroad. Felton should be advised of the latest developments in the conspiracy. Then he must find someone who can get word to Mr. Judd that the detective is in town and wants to see him.

The Presidential Special reaches Newark promptly at 9:30 A.M. The streets are filled with shouting spectators despite near blizzard conditions. At the scheduled stops at Elizabeth, Rahway, and New Brunswick, Mr. Lincoln makes rear-platform appearances. The train slows down as it nears Princeton while hundreds of students watch; their lusty skyrocketing cheers bring a smile to the face of the President-elect as he bows to the college men lining the railroad tracks.

By the time the train arrives in Trenton at ten minutes to twelve, the snow has stopped, and the sun shines brightly on the gaily decorated city. Bands are playing, and thousands shout approval as the Presidential procession moves up State Street to the capitol. Alighting from the carriage, Mr. Lincoln is ushered into the senate chamber. To the presiding officer's welcome, he responds:

"May I be pardoned if, upon this occasion, I mention that way back in my childhood . . . I got hold of a small book, such a one as few of the younger men here have ever seen, Weems' *Life of Washington*. I remember all the accounts . . . of the battle-fields and struggles for the liberties of this country, and none fixed themselves upon my imagination so deeply as the one here at Trenton, New Jersey.

"The crossing of the river, the contest with the Hessians, the great hardships endured at that time . . . I recollect thinking then, boy even though I was, that

there must have been something more than common that these men struggled for . . . I am exceedingly anxious that this Union, the Constitution, and the liberties of the people shall be perpetuated in accordance with the original idea for which that struggle was made. . . ."

Amid wild acclaim Mr. Lincoln is conducted across the hall to the crowded assembly chamber where he is introduced by the Speaker of the House. Again he is loudly cheered, and he acknowledges the introduction by saying:

"Mr. Speaker, the man does not live who is more devoted to peace than I am. . . . But it may be necessary to put the foot down firmly, and if I do my duty . . . and you think I am right, you will stand by me, will you not?"

"We will, we will," shout the legislators, clapping and stamping.

Quietly Mr. Lincoln adds: "That is all I ask."

While the President-elect is addressing the New Jersey legislature in Trenton, the United States Senate is also in session. Sitting in the gallery watching the proceedings is Frederick Seward, son of Senator William H. Seward of New York. A page taps him on the shoulder and whispers that his father wants to see him at once. Slipping from his seat, the young man rushes to the lobby. Senator Seward is waiting, his face grave. He tells his son that he has just received a disturbing report from General Winfield Scott. Evidence points to the fact that the President-elect is in very real danger.

"I want you to go by the first train," the senator says in a low voice. "Find Mr. Lincoln wherever he is. Let no one know your errand. I have written him that I think he should change his arrangements and pass through Baltimore at a different hour. I know it may occasion some embarrassment, and perhaps some ill-natured talk. Nevertheless, I would strongly advise him to do it."

Frederick nods in agreement, tucks the letters into an inside coat pocket, and hurries away to buy a railroad ticket for Philadelphia. He has no idea when he will get an interview with the President-elect, but he realizes how important this mission is. He *must* see Mr. Lincoln somehow.

As soon as the members of the Presidential party have eaten a quick buffet lunch at the Trenton House, they are hustled off to the waiting train. At half past two, right on schedule, the Special heads out through South Trenton, across the Delaware River, and into Pennsylvania. Ninety minutes later it brakes to a halt at the Kensington depot of the Philadelphia and Trenton Railroad.

There Mr. Lincoln is met by local and state dignitaries who escort him to a waiting carriage, stationed at the head of a long procession. The cavalcade of vehicles, police, and militia parades slowly through the packed streets, the President-elect smiling and waving to the enthusiastic crowds.

On the sidewalk near the Continental Hotel, a

young man is waiting, eyeing the occupants of the carriages as they pass. Suddenly he spots the Honorable Norman Judd and breaks through the police guard. Before an officer can grab him, he thrusts a slip of paper into Judd's hand and disappears into the crowd. Furtively Judd glances at the message. It reads: "ST. LOUIS HOTEL, ASK FOR J. H. HUTCHINSON." He sighs with relief; Allan Pinkerton must have come to Philadelphia.

The Presidential carriage draws up at the entrance of the Continental Hotel. In spite of police precautions, the street is clogged with citizens who surge around the vehicle. Colonel Lamon thrusts out both elbows and exerts strong physical pressure to get Mr. Lincoln into the hotel.

After a welcome from the mayor and a hurried meal, the President-elect goes down to the reception parlor to greet the hundreds who have gathered to shake his hand. Not only state dignitaries and city officials but people of every description file by in endless succession.

"God bless you, Abe," says one.

"Do the best you can for us, old fellow!" pleads another.

To each the guest of honor gives a hearty handclasp, nodding and smiling at those who speak to him. He is especially gratified by the remark of one grizzled old man, "You are our only hope, Mr. Lincoln."

17 A PLOT REVEALED
★ Thursday, February 21, 1861 ★

While Mr. Lincoln is holding his reception, Norman Judd pushes his way through the crowded street in an attempt to reach the St. Louis Hotel. It is shortly after seven o'clock when he knocks on the door of the room assigned to J. H. Hutchinson.

Allan Pinkerton answers and greets his old friend warmly. The detective then introduces Mr. Felton, who has been with him all afternoon. The railroad president explains how rumors of plans to destroy his company's property had prompted him to engage Pinkerton and his operatives. Now they have uncovered a conspiracy to kill the President-elect.

Judd wants to know more about Pinkerton's sources of information. Carefully the detective reviews the evidence, step by step. He concludes by saying that he feels the greatest danger lies with a few dedicated men who look upon sacrificing their lives for the Southern cause as a kind of "honored martyrdom." There is no doubt in his mind that these secessionists will attempt to murder Mr. Lincoln if and when he travels through Baltimore.

Before Pinkerton has finished talking, Judd is thoroughly convinced that the President-elect faces great danger if he follows his present schedule. Mr. Lincoln knows nothing of the conspiracy. Judd has kept silent, just as the detective had warned him to do, but now—in the face of all this evidence—the President-elect must be told. A plan must be proposed to insure that he will reach Washington in safety.

The three men talk over various possibilities. They decide the wisest course is for the President-elect to slip out of the city tonight and take the sleeper to Washington. Judd asks Pinkerton to accompany him to the Continental Hotel, where they will disclose the plot to Mr. Lincoln.

It takes nearly an hour for the two men to get through the crowds. The hotel entrance is completely blocked by people. Buffeted back and forth, they finally manage to reach the rear door of the Continental and go directly to Judd's room.

The public reception downstairs ends after two hours, and Mr. Lincoln returns to his rooms, completely worn out. Hearing the crowds in the hallway, Judd surmises the reception is over and immediately sends word to the Presidential suite. He must see Mr. Lincoln at once on a matter of great importance. Tired though he is, the President-elect knows his old friend well, knows he would not ask this favor unless it was imperative. Ten minutes later he enters Judd's room.

While shaking hands with Allan Pinkerton, Mr. Lincoln recalls that he met the detective some years ago during a railroad lawsuit in which both were involved. The three men then sit down, and Judd comes straight to the point. Pinkerton, he explains, has been hired to track down rumors that the Philadelphia, Wilmington and Baltimore Railroad may be sabotaged. During the course of this investigation, the detective has discovered something far more serious—a plot to assassinate the President-elect.

Mr. Lincoln listens intently, his head bowed, but says nothing. After Judd has finished, Pinkerton discusses the activities of Ferrandina, the Baltimore leader of the conspiracy, and describes the way in which the assassins were chosen by secret ballot. The detective also stresses that Police Marshal Kane is involved with the pro-Southern group, that no police protection can be expected when the Presidential party reaches the city. He reminds Mr. Lincoln that even a friendly crowd can be dangerous because of its very size. What happened in Albany is evidence of that fact. If there is not some change in the travel plans, Pinkerton is convinced the plot will be carried through.

The President-elect is silent for a few moments, stunned by the implications of the conspiracy just revealed to him. Judd suggests that he and Pinkerton have worked out a plan whereby the President-elect can leave Philadelphia tonight and be in Washington early tomorrow morning.

Slowly Mr. Lincoln raises his head. "No, I cannot consent to this," he says quietly. "I shall hoist the flag on Independence Hall tomorrow morning and go to Harrisburg tomorrow. Then I have fulfilled all my engagements, and if you, Judd, and you, Allan, think there is positive danger in my attempting to go through Baltimore openly according to the published program—if you can arrange any way to carry out your views, I shall endeavor to get away quietly from the people at Harrisburg tomorrow evening and shall place myself in your hands."

The firmness of Mr. Lincoln's voice convinces his listeners that to argue further is hopeless. Judd turns to Pinkerton and asks how they should proceed. The detective replies that if the President-elect can leave Harrisburg tomorrow night without being observed, a special train will return him to Philadelphia in time to catch the sleeper for Washington. The likelihood of being recognized in Baltimore during the early morning hours is quite remote.

Details of the proposed plan are thoroughly discussed. Mr. Lincoln is worried about his family. Will they be in any danger if they continue on the scheduled journey? The detective reassures him. It is only the President-elect that the conspirators want to harm, he says. Pinkerton will make all the

arrangements; he stresses the importance of complete secrecy being maintained. Mr. Lincoln cannot agree. He must tell his wife. And, he adds, it is probable that she will insist Colonel Lamon accompany him—she has such faith in his former law partner. Other than Mrs. Lincoln, however, he promises to tell no one.

Shortly after eleven the President-elect goes to his suite. A visitor is waiting—a young man who introduces himself as Frederick Seward, the son of Senator William H. Seward. He hands Mr. Lincoln the communications he has brought from his father. Silently the President-elect reads:

Washington, Feb. 21st

My dear Sir,

   My son goes express to you—he will show you a report made by our detective to General Scott—and by him communicated to me this morning. I deem it so important as to dispatch my son to meet you wherever he may find you—I concur with Genl. Scott in thinking it best for you to reconsider your arrangements. No one here but Genl. Scott, myself & the bearer is aware of this communication.

   I should have gone with it myself but for the peculiar sensitiveness about my attendance in the Senate at this crisis.

Very truly yours
William H. Seward

Mr. Lincoln's face does not change expression. He opens the second letter and learns that General Scott has been informed of threats and violence; there are plans to assassinate the President-elect as he passes through Baltimore. Such risks, insists the general, can be avoided if the traveling arrangements are changed. He urges this be done.

After a long silence, Mr. Lincoln asks if Frederick knows how this information was obtained. The young man shakes his head.

"I may as well tell you why I ask," explains the President-elect. "There were stories or rumors some time ago, before I left home, about people who were intending to do me a mischief. I never attached much importance to them—never wanted to believe any such thing. So I never would do anything about them, in the way of taking precautions and the like.

"Some of my friends, though, thought differently," Mr. Lincoln continues, "Judd and others— and without my knowledge they employed a detective to look into the matter. It seems he has occasionally reported what he found, and only today, since we arrived at this house, he brought this story, or something similar to it, about an attempt on my life in the confusion and hurly-burly of the reception at Baltimore."

"Surely," says young Seward, "that is a strong corroboration of the news I brought you."

Mr. Lincoln smiles sadly. "That is exactly why I am asking you about names. If different persons, not knowing of each other's work, have been pursuing separate clues that led to the same result, why then it shows there may be something to it. . . ."

A look of relief crosses the young man's face. Undoubtedly the President-elect will now change his plans. Mr. Lincoln, as if reading Seward's thoughts, says that it is late now and he needs more time to think the matter over. He will let Frederick know what his decision is in the morning.

The messenger is obviously disappointed. He had hoped his father's communications would be persuasion enough. What he doesn't know—and Mr. Lincoln cannot tell him—is that a decision has already been made. The plans "will be changed," but he has promised Allan Pinkerton to tell no one except his wife. The President-elect cannot break that promise.

18 FLAG RAISING OVER INDEPENDENCE HALL
★ Friday, February 22, 1861 ★

During the early morning hours of this twelfth day of the inaugural journey, Allan Pinkerton completes his plans to outwit the conspirators in Baltimore. Mr. Felton offers to arrange the special train that will leave Harrisburg tonight and take Mr. Lincoln back to Philadelphia. The President-elect will then travel incognito on the regularly scheduled sleeper to Washington, arriving at 6 A.M. tomorrow morning. All telegraph wires leading out of the Pennsylvania capital will be temporarily shut off; no messages concerning the sudden change in plans will reach the outside world.

It is almost daylight by the time all the details have been settled. The detective hails a hack and asks to be driven back to the St. Louis Hotel. The sky is clear; there's promise of good weather ahead. Already people are beginning to gather around Independence Hall where this morning the incoming President will raise the American flag. The flag is new to Philadelphia—and new to the nation. Its thirty-fourth star represents the admission of the free state of Kansas to the Union less than a month ago. The citizenry feels proud that this city has been honored by such a momentous event.

A little before seven o'clock, Mr. Lincoln leaves the Continental Hotel. His escort is the Scott Legion, made up of men who fought in the War with Mexico. Preceded by their military band, the President-elect is conducted through swarming crowds to the red-brick building on Chestnut Street. Theodore L. Cuyler, president of the city's Select Council, welcomes him to Independence Hall. Inside the white-paneled assembly room where the Declaration of Independence was signed, Mr. Lincoln remains silent for a few moments, awed by patriotic memories. Turning to face the distinguished guests gathered here, he says:

"I am filled with deep emotion at finding myself standing here in the place where were collected together the wisdom, the patriotism, the devotion to principle, from which spring the institutions under which we live. . . . I have never had a feeling politically that did not spring from the sentiments embodied in the Declaration of Independence.

"I have often pondered over the dangers which were incurred by the men who assembled here and adopted that Declaration of Independence—I have pondered over the toils that were endured by the officers and soldiers of the army who achieved that Independence.

"I have often inquired of myself, what great principle or idea it was that kept this Confederacy so long together. It was not the mere matter of the separation of the colonies from the motherland; but something in that Declaration giving liberty not alone to the people of this country, but hope to the world for all future time.

"It was that which gave promise that in due time all the weights should be lifted from the shoulders of all men, and that *all* should have an equal chance. That is the sentiment embodied in that Declaration of Independence.

"Now, my friends, can this country be saved upon that basis? If it can, I will consider myself one of the happiest men in the world if I can help to save it. If it can't be saved upon that principle, it will be truly awful. But, if this country cannot be saved without giving up that principle—I was about to say I would rather be assassinated on this spot than to surrender it. . . ."

Mr. Lincoln ends by stating that he had not intended to make a speech. This is "wholly unprepared," but, he adds, "I have said nothing but what I am willing to live by, and, in the pleasure of Almighty God, die by."

Applause fills the room, and many of the guests come forward to pay their respects. After a brief tour of the building, the Presidential party goes outside. The appearance of Mr. Lincoln occasions prolonged shouts and cheering from the crowd massed in Chestnut Street. He mounts the platform erected for the occasion in front of Independence Hall and is introduced by Stephen Benton, chairman of the Committee on City Property.

Looking out over the sea of faces, the President-elect begins:

> "I am invited before you to participate in raising above Independence Hall the flag of our country with an additional star upon it. . . . When that flag was originally raised here it had but thirteen stars . . . each additional star added to that flag has given additional prosperity and happiness to this country until it has advanced to its present condition; and its welfare in the future, as well as in the past, is in your hands. . . .
>
> "I think we may promise ourselves that not only the new star placed upon the flag shall be permitted to remain there to our permanent prosperity for years to come, but additional ones shall from time to time be placed there, until we shall number as was anticipated by the great historian, five hundred millions of happy and prosperous people."

After a short prayer delivered by a Philadelphia clergyman, Mr. Lincoln steps over to the flagstaff and grasps the halyard. Pulling hand over hand, he hoists up the tightly rolled bundle. Just as the flag reaches the top of the pole, it is caught by a sudden breeze. The silken folds unfurl, revealing the beauty of the Stars and Stripes, and the crowd cheers.

While these ceremonies are taking place at Independence Hall, Allan Pinkerton gets in touch with Mrs. Warne. He explains to her the changes that have taken place within the last few hours. Her assignment is to be at the Philadelphia, Wilmington and Baltimore station tonight, packed and

ready to leave. She is to play the part of an "anxious sister" waiting to accompany her ailing brother on the train to Washington. Get there early, Pinkerton advises, and buy four tickets on the 10:50 P.M. express to Washington.

Because the departure time for the Special has been set for 9 A.M., the Presidential party hastens back to the Continental Hotel immediately after the flag-raising ceremony. Detective Pinkerton is waiting in the lobby and signals Norman Judd that he wants a word with him in private. The two men meet in Judd's room, and Pinkerton says that all the plans are now complete. Try to get Mr. Lincoln away from the governor's dinner tonight as inconspicuously as possible, he advises, and tell only those who *must* know what is going to happen. Judd nods his head and wishes the detective luck as the two shake hands in parting.

Hurrying down the hallway, Judd raps at the door of the Presidential suite. Mr. Lincoln has just arrived and found Frederick Seward waiting for him. After the necessary introductions, the President-elect explains that Senator Seward sent his son to Philadelphia yesterday to warn about the same conspiracy that Pinkerton described. Mr. Lincoln suggests that Norman Judd tell Frederick "in so far as you think fit" what has now been decided.

Without revealing any details, Judd explains that arrangements have been made to get Mr. Lin-

coln safely to Washington. He can say no more.
Thanking the two gentlemen, Frederick hastens
out to a nearby telegraph office. He will send his
father the code word the two have agreed upon in
order to reassure the senator.

19 SUSPENSE
★ Friday, February 22, 1861 ★

Cannon are booming and bands playing when
the line of carriages bearing the Presidential party
draws up at the Pennsylvania Railroad station in
West Philadelphia. The cheering thousands gathered here make no attempt to waylay the President-elect as he walks to the waiting train. When
everyone is aboard, the Special leaves promptly
on schedule.

Norman Judd enters the rear coach and asks for
a few words alone with Mr. Lincoln. In a low
whisper Judd explains that Pinkerton spoke to him
just before they left the hotel, that arrangements
have been completed for tonight's journey. The
President-elect listens carefully, his face serious.
The two men agree that Colonel Sumner, Major
Hunter, Captain Hazzard, and Captain Pope
should be told, in addition to Colonel Lamon and
Judge Davis. Perhaps after the ceremonies at Harrisburg would be the best time.

Today's trip follows much the same pattern as

the preceding rides have. Stops are made at Haverford, Paoli, Downingtown, and Coatesville where Mr. Lincoln makes his usual appearance on the rear platform and says a few words to the crowds that surround the Special. After a short speech at Leaman Place, there are loud calls for Mrs. Lincoln. The President-elect reenters the coach and returns with his smiling wife. Introducing her to the people, he says he wants to give them "the long and short of it." There are bursts of laughter and hearty cheers as the train pulls out.

People in Lancaster, Elizabethtown, Mount Joy, and Middleburg all have the opportunity to see Mr. Lincoln before the Special arrives in Harrisburg at half past one. Crowds in the state capital —both civilians and military—are out in full force to greet the President-elect. Mr. Lincoln is escorted to the Jones House on Market Square where Governor Andrew Curtin welcomes him. From the hotel portico, the President-elect makes a short speech, complimenting the military companies that are standing at attention by saying they are "the finest" he has ever seen. Then he continues:

". . . allow me to express the hope that in the shedding of blood their services may never be needed. . . . It shall be my endeavour to preserve the peace of this country so far as it can possibly be done, consistently with the maintenance of the institutions of the country."

After a luncheon at the Jones House, Mr. Lincoln is driven to the Pennsylvania state capitol where he addresses the combined legislative bodies. He speaks of having raised the new flag at Independence Hall and adds:

". . . I could not help hoping that there was in the entire success of that beautiful ceremony, at least something of an omen of what is to come."

After the Presidential party has returned to the hotel, Norman Judd summons Governor Curtin, the four army officers, Colonel Lamon, and Judge Davis to Mr. Lincoln's suite. (Governor Curtin has been included because his cooperation will be needed.) Only after pledging the gentlemen to secrecy does Judd describe the Baltimore plot and tell them how Pinkerton proposes to outwit the conspirators.

When he reveals the plans for tonight's escape to Washington, one of the army officers blusters out that this will be "a damned piece of cowardice." Judd counters that Mr. Lincoln and he have already considered the possibility that the President-elect may be subjected to ridicule; nevertheless, the plan will be carried out in order to avoid a danger far greater than scorn or laughter.

Mr. Lincoln, silent up to this moment, explains that he has told no one except his wife and that she has insisted that Colonel Lamon accompany him tonight. Judd announces that the rest of the Presidential party will continue the trip exactly as scheduled. Now the men take their leave, shaking their heads in disbelief that this triumphant inaugural journey must end in such a secretive climax.

Dinner tonight is a festive occasion, with Governor Curtin the host and Mr. Lincoln the honored guest. Midway through the meal John Nicolay enters the dining room with a prearranged message for the President-elect. Mr. Lincoln rises and leaves abruptly. Governor Curtin, Colonel Lamon, and Norman Judd follow.

Hurrying to his suite, the President-elect pulls on his old overcoat; instead of the tall silk stovepipe so familiar to the public, he takes the soft wool hat given to him in New York City, stuffing it into his overcoat pocket. Tossing a shawl over his arm, Mr. Lincoln picks up the small gripsack and leaves the suite accompanied by the governor.

Norman Judd and Colonel Lamon are waiting beside the carriage at the side entrance to the hotel. Mr. Lincoln gives Judd a quick handshake and climbs into the carriage, followed by the governor and Colonel Lamon. The driver heads out toward the city limits, rather than to the railroad station. On a lone siding is a locomotive with a baggage car and one passenger coach attached. The engineer has been told he is to take some railroad officials back to Philadelphia. Because the baggage car blocks his rear view, he will never know the identity of his passengers.

Governor Curtin bids Mr. Lincoln a hasty farewell as the President-elect and Colonel Lamon leave the carriage. Lamon strides toward the locomotive cab and tells the engineer that he may start his run in two minutes flat. Then the two lone passengers enter the coach through the rear-platform door and settle themselves for the trip to Philadelphia.

Back at the Jones House Norman Judd explains that Mr. Lincoln has been taken ill. In view of the stress of the past twelve days—the speeches, the handshaking, the traveling—this does not seem surprising. Members of the Presidential party at the governor's reception tonight remind each other of how much Mr. Lincoln has had to endure during the journey. It is no wonder he is sick. The few who know otherwise keep silent.

Meanwhile, the train bearing the President-elect and his companion speeds across Pennsylvania, stopping only once to take on water at Downingtown. The engineer makes good time. There is nothing ahead to slow him down, and no other train will follow on this track tonight. Allan Pinkerton is waiting at the West Philadelphia station as the train pulls in—twenty-seven minutes ahead of schedule.

Watching the rear coach, the detective has an anxious moment as the two men come into view. Mr. Lincoln, wearing the soft wool hat instead of his usual stovepipe, is difficult to recognize. But this is all to the good, Pinkerton decides, as he greets the travelers. The three men get into a carriage, and Pinkerton directs the hackman to drive to the Philadelphia, Wilmington and Baltimore station.

Mrs. Kate Warne has reached the depot an hour

earlier and purchased the tickets. Because her chief instructed her to reserve the last four berths in the rear car, she immediately went to the waiting sleeper. Sleeping-car tickets are not numbered, and passengers may choose from whatever berths are available. Mrs. Warne enlisted the help of the conductor, telling him that "a sick brother" is coming aboard and she must have the last four berths. He helped her hold these while she talked about her "brother" and how worried she is over his condition.

At five minutes before the scheduled departure time of 10:50 P.M., Pinkerton, Lamon, and their distinguished passenger enter the depot. There are no protective shadows; they must walk through the glaring light of the station. Pinkerton, grasping

Mr. Lincoln's elbow, insists that he keep his head down, let his shoulders droop. With the shawl pulled around him, he is to simulate an aged, ill man.

Colonel Lamon, who is heavily armed, follows a few feet behind; to anyone watching, however, he appears to be alone. The other passengers in the station take no notice of the feeble old man being helped on to the train. Though outwardly calm, Pinkerton looks furtively about, watching for any danger that may arise unexpectedly.

Mr. Lincoln's entrance into the sleeping car has been perfectly timed; the moment he steps aboard, the train starts to move. Mrs. Warne greets her "aged brother" and guides him to the berth he is to occupy. She plays her role well; the few passengers who observe this bit of acting are impressed with her solicitous care.

As he pulls the curtains of the berth together, Mr. Lincoln realizes he is very tired. He finds the space too short to accommodate his long legs. He tries stretching out from corner to corner, tries doubling his legs and feet beneath him. Despite his fatigue, the President-elect is unable to sleep.

Across the aisle, Pinkerton reviews the events of the past few hours. Has someone recognized Mr. Lincoln when they walked through the station? Have the conspirators in Baltimore been alerted to the fact that the man they want to murder is now on his way toward their city? The trip

from Harrisburg—on a special train with all the
telegraph wires grounded—was relatively safe.
But this part of the journey is different. There are
so many hidden dangers. Will their stratagem
work? Pinkerton wonders.

20 DESTINATION: WASHINGTON, D.C.
★ Saturday, February, 23, 1861 ★

There's a rhythmic clack-clack of wheels punctuated by the intermittent wail of the locomotive's whistle as the train rushes through the early morning hours on this the thirteenth day of the journey. Each mile brings new hazards. Allan Pinkerton has exercised every precaution, has stationed secret agents along the route with instructions to flash a quick signal if everything is all right. Still, the detective cannot smother his fears altogether.

As the train nears Havre de Grace, Maryland, he becomes increasingly apprehensive. It is here where the individual railroad cars must be taken across the Susquehanna River by ferryboat and reassembled on the opposite shore that there may be critical moments of danger.

Pinkerton leaves his berth and goes to the rear platform, his eyes searching the darkness for the expected signal that all is well. Within seconds, there's a flash of light in the distance. The detective sighs with relief and returns to the coach, whispering to Mr. Lincoln that they have arrived in Havre de Grace and so far everything is going as planned.

After the ferryboats have transferred the cars and the train begins rolling again, Pinkerton becomes more and more tense. Every crossing, every bridge, every town as they near Baltimore, are filled with potential threats. He walks to the rear platform at frequent intervals, watching for his agents to signal.

At 3:30 A.M. the train begins losing momentum as it approaches the Calvert Street station in Baltimore. This is the critical hour; this is the city where the murder has been plotted to take place. Has Ferrandina somehow learned of Mr. Lincoln's presence in this coach? Is one of the conspirators even now waiting to strike?

Once the train comes to a halt, Mrs. Warne leaves her berth and whispers good-bye to her three fellow passengers. Her role of "solicitous sister" is over. Accompanying her to a carriage, Pinkerton tells her to check in at a hotel and report any new developments. He'll be particularly anxious to hear Baltimore's reaction when the Presidential Special arrives today at 12:30 P.M.

Now the passenger cars are being uncoupled. Because there is no single station to serve all the railroad lines that enter the city, the coaches of this Philadelphia, Wilmington and Baltimore train must be detached from the locomotive and hauled across town by dray horses. They will then be attached to a Baltimore and Ohio locomotive at the Camden station and proceed to Washington.

This is the time Pinkerton dreads most. Assailants, lurking in side streets, could easily surround and attack the railroad car. The detective cautions Mr. Lincoln that under no circumstances must he leave his berth. It is only a matter of minutes before the passenger car begins moving, this time hitched to a team of horses.

The staccato sound of hoofs echoes through the deserted streets as the coach is towed through the city. Again Allan Pinkerton peers anxiously from the rear platform; every shadow seems to present a menace. Across the aisle from Mr. Lincoln, Colonel Lamon listens for any suspicious sound; his hand on his holster, he is ready to leap into action should need arise.

The passenger cars reach the Camden station without incident and are coupled to the Baltimore and Ohio locomotive. Once reassembled, the train still does not move. The three men in the rear sleeper can hear people milling about outside, laughing and singing. A noisy rendition of "Dixey's Land" is cheered.

Minutes drag by. Pinkerton cannot understand the delay. He hunts up the conductor and learns they are waiting for passengers coming in on a train from the west. That train is late; there's no indication how soon it will arrive. Though Mr. Lincoln remains strangely calm, the detective's nervousness mounts. Are the conspirators waiting for a prearranged signal to rush in and attack the President-elect?

Nearly an hour elapses before there's a noisy commotion in the aisle. The delayed passengers are bursting through the coach, looking for vacant berths. At last the conductor calls "All aboard," and the train gets under way. Pinkerton remains tense. It is just possible that one of these late arrivals has been designated as the assassin. Yet only the shrill locomotive whistle pierces the silence.

Darkness has given way to early morning light when the train lurches to a stop in the Union Station in Washington. Mr. Lincoln, stiff from the tedious journey, unwinds his long legs and eases himself out of his berth. Colonel Lamon and Allan Pinkerton are already in the aisle, waiting for their passenger. The President-elect digs out the soft wool hat from his overcoat pocket. Pulling it down around his ears, he wraps the shawl about his shoulders and grins at his companions. The three men move to the forward end of the coach, then step onto the train platform.

Pinkerton scans the crowd carefully. There are many people, but everyone seems intent on his own business. He is confident they can make their way through the depot without being recognized. Colonel Lamon walks alongside Mr. Lincoln, the detective a few feet behind. Suddenly Pinkerton spots a man staring at the President-elect and defensively steps forward. But the stranger has already grabbed Mr. Lincoln's hand. "Abe," he exclaims, "you can't do this to me."

As Colonel Lamon reaches for his pistol, the detective throws out his left elbow, and the man staggers back. Quickly recovering himself, he again reaches for Mr. Lincoln's arm, proclaiming that he is a friend. Pinkerton, assuming this is the attack they have feared, clenches his fist and raises his arm.

Mr. Lincoln grabs the detective. "Don't strike him, Allan, don't strike him—this is my friend Washburne—don't you know him?"

Congressman Elihu B. Washburne of Illinois is well acquainted with the President-elect. Senator Seward has confided in Washburne, explaining how the schedule has been changed. Mr. Lincoln, he has surmised, will arrive at six o'clock this morning on the sleeper; Washburne has come to the Union Station to welcome his old friend.

Pinkerton apologizes for his defensive behavior. He's never met the congressman, he explains. Washburne laughingly admits he should have been more cautious. Frowning at the loud talk, the detective warns them all to say nothing that will attract attention as they walk through the station. When they reach the street, Washburne hails a carriage and directs the driver to Willard's Hotel.

Still anxious about his passenger, Pinkerton orders the driver to stop a short distance from the hotel. The detective, Mr. Lincoln, and Washburne get out and walk toward the ladies' entrance.

Lamon is instructed to go on to the main lobby.
He finds Mr. Willard and brings him to meet the
other three just inside the door. The hotelkeeper
apologizes. Suite 6 is not yet prepared—Mr. Lincoln was not expected for several hours. But he
may have another room to use for the present.

The President-elect thanks Pinkerton for all his
work and begs to be excused. He has had no sleep
for twenty-four hours and retires, thoroughly exhausted. The detective checks in at the hotel desk,
registering as "E. J. Allen." Before going to his
room, he looks up the nearest telegraph office.

To Norman Judd in Harrisburg, he sends the following dispatch:

> Arrived here all right.

Using the secret code, he informs his superintendent in Chicago:

> Plum has nuts—arri'd at Barley—all right.

(Decoded, this reads, "Pinkerton has President
—arrived at Washington all right.")

It is shortly after 8 A.M. in the Pennsylvania
capital when Norman Judd receives the telegram.
Members of the Presidential party have been worrying about whether Mr. Lincoln will be well
enough today to make the trip to Washington.
When Judd circulates the news, there is surprise
and consternation. Some are angered because they
have not been informed of the counterplot. It's
a momentous "scoop" for the reporters; they rush

out to file their stories on the wire service which has now been restored.

The Special leaves Harrisburg an hour later with the Presidential party aboard. Pinkerton in his room at the Willard Hotel fervently hopes that his judgment has been correct, that there will be no trouble at noon in Baltimore. He has told Mr. Lincoln that the plotters want only the President-elect; the rest of the party will be perfectly safe.

Long before the Special is due, an ill-humored crowd of about fifteen thousand is massed around the Calvert Street Station. Because Maryland is a slave state and Baltimore its largest city, the militant group of Southern sympathizers is very vocal here. Hatred, discontent and suspicion toward the federal government is rampant.

When the train arrives in Baltimore at 12:30 P.M., there is a mad rush for the Special. The mob overruns the station and swarms out to the platform, surrounding the coaches. Raucous cheers are heard—three for the Southern Confederacy, three for "gallant Jeff Davis," and three groans for "the Rail Splitter." Marshal Kane's police force is nowhere in evidence.

Faces peer into the windows shouting threats and insults: "Come out, old Abe!" "Let's have him out!" "We'll give you Hell!" Some attempt to enter the coach where Mrs. Lincoln and the boys are sitting, but John Hay pushes the intruders back and bolts the door. There is wild confusion everywhere.

Nearly an hour passes before Mrs. Lincoln and her sons can be escorted to the waiting carriage without danger of assault. Rather than driving to the Eutaw House as previously planned, the family of the President-elect is taken to the home of John S. Gittings, a director of the Baltimore and Ohio Railroad. Mr. Wood, who is in charge of the Special, spots a large omnibus nearby and hires the driver to transport the rest of the party to the hotel. Rowdies follow behind, shouting insults and abuse.

Two hours later the passengers are driven to the Camden Street Station to board the Special for Washington. Here another mob is waiting, not so large but fully as insulting. Once Mrs. Lincoln and her sons reach the safety of the rear coach, rough-looking men shout foul invectives; some even try to pry open the train windows.

Now the police arrive and attempt to restore order. Eventually they manage to clear a small area around the tracks, and the train pulls out of the station, leaving behind a tense situation that borders on riot.

Rain is falling when the Presidential Special comes into the station at the corner of New Jersey Avenue and C Street. The passengers are relieved to have finally arrived in the national capital. Senator Seward is waiting to greet Mr. Lincoln's family and drive them to the Willard Hotel.

In Suite 6 the President-elect has just said good-bye to a Congressional delegation when Willie and

Tad burst through the door followed by Mrs. Lincoln and Robert. For a moment the tension and strife of a nation in crisis are forgotten. The long journey is over . . . the family is together again. A grateful smile spreads across Mr. Lincoln's drawn face.

Epilogue

Mr. Lincoln's secret journey from Harrisburg to Washington was front-page news for many days. Distorted versions appeared in leading newspapers all over this country and abroad. From Harrisburg on the morning of February 23, Joseph Howard, Jr., a reporter for *The New York Times,* filed a dispatch about the sudden departure of the President-elect, concluding with the sentence: "He wore a Scotch plaid cap and a very long military cloak, so that he was entirely unrecognizable."

Stories in a responsible paper like *The Times,* known to be friendly to Mr. Lincoln, were accepted as true. Thousands of papers reprinted the false report of his disguise in news items and editorial comments. The cartoonists went wild, exaggerating how the lanky President-elect had tiptoed into the capital in cloak and plaid cap.

On Monday morning, February 25, the *New York Tribune* explained that Lincoln's early arrival was caused "solely by an official communication from

General Scott, predicated upon sufficient information which he had received of the danger of a
riot at Baltimore, and probably of a desperate de-
termination at assault on the route. . . . While Mr.
Lincoln entertained no apprehensions for his own
safety, he did not feel justified in hazarding the
public peace. His decision was, therefore, made
in respect to the judgment of the War Department,
and upon a state of facts of which he could have
no personal knowledge."

The *Baltimore Sun,* however, editorialized: "Had
we any respect for Mr. Lincoln, official or personal, as a man, or as President-elect of the United
States, his career and speeches on his way to the
seat of government would have cruelly impaired
it; but the final escapade by which he reached
the capital would have utterly demolished it, and
overwhelmed us with mortification. . . . We do not
believe the Presidency can ever be more degraded
by any of his successors, than it has been by him,
even before his inauguration; and so, for aught we
care, he may go to the full extent of his wretched
comicalities."

The Albany *Atlas and Argus* proclaimed: "This
termination of his journey, by a flight under cover
of darkness, disguised in old clothes, is inglorious
and disgraceful." A foreign diplomat wrote his
government that "like a thief in the night, the future President arrived here on the early morning
of the 23rd."

When Allan Pinkerton persuaded Mr. Lincoln

to change his scheduled plans, he warned that the President-elect might be subjected to ridicule from his enemies. The warning was well founded. Even among his friends, there was criticism of the secret journey. Sometime later, Mr. Lincoln told his friend Congressman Isaac N. Arnold of Illinois: "I did not then, nor do I now believe I should have been assassinated had I gone through Baltimore as first contemplated, but I thought it wise to run no risk where no risk was necessary."

The nine days between arrival and inauguration were difficult and tiresome ones for Mr. Lincoln. Hordes of officeseekers called at suite Number 6. There were public appearances to make, important politicians to chat with. The pressure was tremendous, causing the incoming President to say that Springfield was "bad enough . . . but it was child's play compared with this tussle here."

During the early hours of March 4, 1861, leaden clouds filled the sky. A light mist was falling but by mid-morning the sun had broken through for this—Mr. Lincoln's inaugural day. Thousands stood along either side of Pennsylvania Avenue. The mall in front of the Capitol's east portico was packed with people.

In view of the many threats of violence, General Scott had taken every possible precaution. On rooftops overlooking the parade route, he stationed rifle squads. Military troops lined the street, and armed guards were ordered to watch the crowd in front of the Capitol.

Shortly after twelve noon, President Buchanan called for Mr. Lincoln at Willard's Hotel. The two men rode side by side in an open carriage up Pennsylvania Avenue, accompanied by marching groups, floats, and bands. During a brief ceremony in the Senate Chamber, Hannibal Hamlin was sworn in as Vice-President. Then Mr. Lincoln, escorted by President Buchanan, Chief Justice Roger Taney, and a host of dignitaries walked out to the special platform which had been erected on the east front. Behind them was the spreading Capitol with its unfinished dome surmounted by steel derricks.

Senator Edward Baker of Oregon stepped forward. "Fellow citizens," he said, "I introduce to you Abraham Lincoln, the President-elect of the United States." At the edge of the crowd photographer Mathew Brady held up his camera, ready to snap the first picture ever taken of a President reading his inaugural address.

Mr. Lincoln stood up, walked to the podium, and placed his manuscript on it. Pulling out a pair of steel-rimmed spectacles and adjusting them on his nose, he looked out at the throng of twenty thousand. In a loud clear voice he began:

"Fellow citizens of the United States, in compliance with a custom as old as the Government itself, I appear before you to address you briefly, and to take, in your presence, the oath prescribed by the Constitution. . . .

"It is seventy-two years since the first inauguration

of a President under our national Constitution. During that period fifteen different and greatly distinguished citizens have, in succession, administered the executive branch of the Government. They have conducted it through many perils; and, generally, with great success. Yet, with all this scope for precedent, I now enter upon the same task . . . under great and peculiar difficulty. A disruption of the Federal Union heretofore only menaced, is now formidably attempted. . . .

"I shall take care as the Constitution itself expressly enjoins upon me, that the laws of the Union be faithfully executed in all the States. . . .

"This country, with its institutions, belongs to the people who inhabit it. . . . In our present difference, is either party without faith of being in the right? . . ."

Mr. Lincoln paused for a moment. Then addressing the Southerners, he continued:

"In your hands, my dissatisfied fellow countrymen, and not in mine, is the momentous issue of civil war. The Government will not assail you. You can have no conflict, without being yourselves the aggressors. You have no oath registered in Heaven to destroy the Government, while I shall have the most solemn one to 'preserve, protect, and defend it.'

"I am loth to close. We are not enemies, but friends. We must not be enemies. Though passion may have strained, it must not break our bonds of affection. The mystic chords of memory, stretching from every battlefield, and patriot grave, to every living heart and hearthstone, all over this broad land, will yet swell the chorus of the Union, when again touched, as surely they will be, by the better angels of our nature."

Bibliography

ANGLE, PAUL M. *Here I Have Lived: A History of Lincoln's Springfield, 1821–1865.* Springfield, Illinois: The Abraham Lincoln Association, 1935.

BARRINGER, WILLIAM E. *A House Dividing: Lincoln as President-Elect.* Springfield, Illinois: The Abraham Lincoln Association, 1945.

BEERS, F. W. *Atlas of New York and Vicinity.* New York: F. W. Beers, A. T. Ellis and G. G. Soule, 1867.

BROWNE, J. II. *The Great Metropolis: A Mirror of New York.* Hartford: American Publishing Company, 1869.

BRYAN, GEORGE S. *The Great American Myth.* New York: Carrick and Evans, 1940.

CAMPBELL, G. MURRAY. "The Lincoln Inaugural and Funeral Trains." *Railway and Locomotive Historical Society Bulletin.* No. 93, pp. 67–72. October, 1955.

COGGESHALL, WILLIAM T. *The Journeys of Abraham Lincoln from Springfield to Washington, 1861, as President-Elect and from Washington to Springfield, 1865, as President Martyred.* Columbus, Ohio: *Ohio State Journal,* 1865.

CRAMER, JOHN HENRY. "Abraham Lincoln Visits with His People." *Ohio State Archaeological and Historical Quarterly,* Volume 57. Columbus, Ohio. January, 1948, pp. 66–78.

CRAMER, JOHN HENRY. "A President-Elect in Western Pennsylvania." Offprint from *Pennsylvania Magazine of History and Biography.* July, 1947.

CUTHBERT, NORMA B., editor. *Lincoln and the Baltimore Plot: From Pinkerton Records and Related Papers.* San Marino, California: The Huntington Library, 1949.

FATOUT, PAUL. "Mr. Lincoln Goes to Washington." *Indiana Magazine of History.* Bloomington, Indiana, 1951. Volume XLVII, pp. 321–332.

HAMILTON, CHARLES, and LLOYD OSTENDORF. *Lincoln in Photographs: An Album of Every Known Pose.* Norman, Oklahoma: University of Oklahoma Press, 1963.

HERTZ, EMANUEL, editor. *Lincoln Talks: A Biography in Anecdote.* New York: The Viking Press, 1939.

HORAN, JAMES D. *Mathew Brady: Historian with a Camera.* New York: Crown Publishers, Inc., 1955.

KIMMEL, STANLEY. *Mr. Lincoln's Washington.* New York: Bramhall House, 1957.

KING, WILLARD L. *Lincoln's Manager: David Davis.* Cambridge, Massachusetts: Harvard University Press, 1960.

KITTLER, GLENN D. *Hail to the Chief: The Inauguration Days of Our Presidents.* Philadelphia: Chilton Books, 1965.

LAVINE, SIGMUND A. *Allan Pinkerton: America's First Private Eye.* New York: Dodd, Mead & Company, 1963.

LEECH, MARGARET. *Reveille in Washington, 1860–1865.* New York: Harper and Brothers, 1941.

LINCOLN, ABRAHAM. *The Collected Works of Abraham Lincoln.* Roy P. Basler, editor. Volume IV. New Brunswick, New Jersey: Rutgers University Press, 1953.

LORANT, STEFAN. *The Life of Abraham Lincoln.* New York: McGraw-Hill, 1954.

McELROY, ROBERT. *Jefferson Davis.* New York: Harper and Brothers, 1937.

MEARNS, DAVID CHAMBERS. *Largely Lincoln.* New York: St. Martin's Press, 1961.

MESERVE, FREDERICK H. *The Photographs of Abraham Lincoln.* New York: Harcourt, Brace, 1944.

MIERS, EARL SCHENCK, editor. *Lincoln Day by Day: A Chronology.* Volume III: 1861–1865. Washington, D.C.: Lincoln Sesquicentennial Commission, 1960.

MITGANG, HERBERT, editor. *Lincoln as They Saw Him.* New York: Rinehart and Company, Inc., 1956.

NICOLAY, HELEN. *Personal Traits of Abraham Lincoln.* New York: The Century Company, 1912.

PINKERTON, ALLAN. *History and Evidence of Passage of Abraham Lincoln from Harrisburg, Pa. to Washington, D.C. on the 22nd and 23rd of February, 1861.* Chicago: Republican Print, 1868.

PINKERTON, ALLAN. *The Spy of the Rebellion.* New York: G. W. Dillingham, Publisher, 1883.

POTTER, JOHN MASON. *13 Desperate Days.* New York: Ivan Obolensky, Inc., 1964.

PRATT, HARRY E., compiler. *Concerning Mr. Lincoln: In Which Abraham Lincoln Is Pictured as He Appeared to Letter Writers of His Time.* Springfield, Illinois: The Abraham Lincoln Association, 1944.

QUARLES, BENJAMIN. *Lincoln and the Negro.* New York: Oxford University Press, 1962.

RANDALL, J. G. *Lincoln the President: Springfield to Gettysburg.* Volume I. New York: Dodd, Mead & Company, 1945.

RANDALL, RUTH PAINTER. *Lincoln's Sons.* Boston: Little, Brown and Company, 1955.

RANDALL, RUTH PAINTER. *Mary Lincoln: Biography of a Marriage.* Boston: Little, Brown and Company, 1953.

SANDBURG, CARL. *Abraham Lincoln: The War Years.* Volume I. New York: Harcourt, Brace and Company, 1939.

SCHWENGEL, FRED, chairman. *Abraham Lincoln Com-*

memoration Ceremony: The 100th Anniversary of His First Inauguration. Washington, D.C.: United States Government Printing Office, 1962.

SEARCHER, VICTOR. Lincoln's Journey to Greatness. Philadelphia: The John C. Winston Company, 1960.

SEGAL, CHARLES M. Conversations with Lincoln. New York: G. P. Putnam's Sons, 1961.

STARR, JOHN, W., JR. Lincoln and the Railroads. New York: Dodd, Mead & Company, 1927.

STRODE, HUDSON. Jefferson Davis: American Patriot. New York: Harcourt, Brace and Company, 1955.

TARBELL, IDA M. The Life of Abraham Lincoln. New York: Lincoln Memorial Association, 1895.

TILTON, CLINT CLAY. Lincoln's Last View of the Illinois Prairies. Privately printed. Danville, Illinois: Interstate Printing Company, 1937.

THOMAS, BENJAMIN P. Abraham Lincoln. New York: Alfred A. Knopf, Inc., 1952.

VAN DEUSEN, GLYNDON G. William Henry Seward. New York: Oxford University Press, 1967.

VILLARD, HENRY. Memoirs of Henry Villard. Volume I: 1835–1862. Boston: Houghton Mifflin and Company, 1904.

WALLACE, IRVING. The Fabulous Showman: The Life and Times of P. T. Barnum. New York: Alfred A. Knopf, Inc., 1959.

WEIK, JESSE W. The Real Lincoln: A Portrait. Boston: Houghton Mifflin and Company, 1922.

WOLDMAN, ALBERT A. Lawyer Lincoln. Boston: Houghton Mifflin and Company, 1936.

NEWSPAPERS FOR FEBRUARY 1861
Albany Atlas and Argus
Baltimore Sun
Buffalo (New York) Morning Express
Charleston Mercury

Cleveland Herald
Cleveland Plain Dealer
Daily Commercial (Cincinnati, Ohio)
New York Herald
The New York Times
New York Tribune
New York World
Philadelphia Inquirer
Pittsburgh Dispatch

Index

About the Author

Mary Kay Phelan's career as a writer began in response to questions from her two young sons. When, after a trip to Washington, she could not find a book that satisfied their demands for more information about the White House, she wrote one herself. And she has continued to write books that bring American history vividly to life. Mrs. Phelan is the author of *Four Days in Philadelphia—1776*, which tells the story of the adoption of the Declaration of Independence; *Midnight Alarm*, an account of Paul Revere's ride; *The Story of the Great Chicago Fire, 1871*; biographies of Florence Sabin and Martha Berry; and three books in the Crowell Holiday Series—*Mother's Day*, *The Fourth of July*, and *Election Day*.

Born in Kansas, Mrs. Phelan was graduated from DePauw University in Indiana and received her master's degree in English from Northwestern. She has worked as an advertising copywriter and is now, with her husband, involved in the production of historical films which are widely used in schools and libraries. The Phelans live in Davenport, Iowa, most of the year but enjoy their frequent travels in this country and in Europe.

About the Illustrator

Richard Cuffari's paintings have been exhibited in several New York galleries. A number of his illustrations have appeared in the American Institute of Graphic Arts design shows and in the Society of Illustrators annual exhibits.

A native of New York, Mr. Cuffari studied at Pratt Institute. He lives in Brooklyn with his wife and four children.